The Practical Guide to Collibra

Building Active Data Governance Programs That Work

Azhar Rahman

This is a work of nonfiction. The information presented is based on the author's professional experience and industry knowledge. While every effort has been made to ensure accuracy, the author and publisher make no warranties and shall not be held liable for any damages arising from the use of this material.

Disclaimer

This book is an independent publication and is not affiliated with, authorized by, sponsored by, or endorsed in any way by Collibra, Inc. The views, opinions, and experiences expressed are solely those of the author and do not represent the views of Collibra or any other organization. Any references to Collibra are for descriptive and educational purposes only.

First published in 2025

Book Map & Cheat Sheet

Chapter 1: Understanding Collibra and Data Governance Fundamentals

- Explains data governance concepts, why Collibra matters.
- Sets foundation: trust, metadata, stewardship, business value.

Instructions: Learn core terms, roles (stewards, owners, consumers), and why governance is more than compliance.

Chapter 2: Planning, Pre-implementation and Readiness Assessment

- Covers readiness checks: people, processes, technology.
- Helps avoid underestimating scope.

Instructions: Run an honest assessment. Identify gaps in sponsorship, skills, and budget before starting.

Chapter 3: How to Design Your Core Meta Model

- Designing the "skeleton" of Collibra (domains, communities, assets).
- Warns against over-engineering.

Instructions: Keep the model lean, aligned to business outcomes. Plan for iteration.

Chapter 4: Establishing Your Governance Operating Model

- Defines roles, ownership, decision rights, escalation paths.
- Pitfalls: overcomplication, unfunded stewardship, mismatched tooling .

Instructions: Document clearly, test with real cases, and revisit quarterly.

Chapter 5: Sprint Planning and Agile Implementation

- Advocates agile over waterfall.
- Core practices: backlog creation, sprint cadence, daily stand-ups, retrospectives .

Instructions: Use 2–3 week sprints. Define goals by user impact, not configuration tasks. Empower Product Owner + Scrum Master.

Chapter 6: Writing Effective User Stories and Acceptance Criteria

- Stories anchor delivery: *As a <persona>, I want <something>, so that <benefit>* .
- Emphasis on personas, splitting stories, crisp acceptance criteria.

Instructions: Coach stewards & stakeholders to write their own stories. Map stories to KPIs. Avoid vague or "endless" stories.

Chapter 7: Team Structure and Stakeholder Engagement

- Governance succeeds on human networks, not org charts .
- Build a small core nucleus, then scale via councils and domain groups.
- Engagement tactics: recognition, career paths, informal connection (even lunch!) .

Instructions: Budget for engagement. Track participation metrics. Treat documentation as a living product.

Chapter 8: Technical Implementation and Configuration

- Covers deployment topologies (SaaS, cloud, on-premise) .
- Security, performance tuning, version control, automation.
- Real-world war stories on scaling, integration, and audits .

Instructions: Focus on making Collibra "useful" not just "installed." Store configurations in version control. Automate tests.

Chapter 9: Data Asset Onboarding and Cataloging

- Turning configuration into value by cataloging assets .
- Importance of consistency, stewardship, lineage, and quality.

Instructions: Start small (key domains first). Balance automation with stewardship review. Avoid "free-for-all" changes.

Chapter 10: Building Workflows and Automation

- Designing approval processes, certifications, notifications.
- Automate repetitive governance tasks.

Instructions: Keep workflows lightweight. Test end-to-end with real stewards. Use automation but maintain clarity in roles.

Chapter 11: Integrating Collibra with Your Data Ecosystem

- API, lineage, and metadata integration with BI, ETL, quality tools.
- Focus on reliability, monitoring, error handling .

Instructions: Prioritize business-value metrics (time-to-catalog, lineage coverage). Assign clear integration owners.

Chapter 12: Change Management and User Adoption

- Adoption is the "main event" .
- Overcomes cultural inertia: people default to old tools unless engaged.
- Strategies: training, recognition, visible executive sponsorship.

Instructions: Run awareness campaigns, measure adoption, celebrate wins. Embed governance in daily work, not as an extra.

Chapter 13: Measuring Success and KPI Development

- KPIs link governance stories to business outcomes (e.g., reduced request cycle time, audit findings).
- Transparency builds trust.

Instructions: Track usage metrics, response times, cycle times, and business impact. Share openly.

Chapter 14: Common Pitfalls and Troubleshooting

- Typical failures: over-engineering, lack of incentives, technical instability, burnout

- Provides rescue tactics and troubleshooting patterns.

Instructions: Watch for red flags (workflow abandonment, vague acceptance criteria). Fix root cause, not just symptoms.

Chapter 15: Scaling and Continuous Improvement

- Governance is never "done."
- Maturing means decentralization, new roles, new use cases.
- Continuous retrospectives and incremental expansion.

Instructions: Treat operating model as versioned. Expand slowly, guided by metrics. Celebrate progress to keep momentum.

How to Use This Cheat Sheet

- **Before starting**: Read Ch.1-4 (foundations).
- **During build**: Use Ch.5-11 as your "playbook."
- **Driving adoption**: Apply Ch.12-13.
- **Sustaining growth**: Revisit Ch.14-15.

Essential Terms for This Book

Core Data Governance

- **Data Governance** – Framework of roles, processes, and policies ensuring trustworthy, well-managed data.
- **Data Steward** – Person responsible for data quality, definitions, and usage.
- **Data Owner** – Senior stakeholder with decision rights and accountability for a dataset/domain.
- **Custodian** – IT role ensuring secure technical storage and delivery of data.
- **Business Glossary** – Repository of agreed business terms and their definitions.
- **Golden Source** – The official, authoritative dataset for a given element.
- **Data Quality** – Measurement of data's accuracy, timeliness, completeness, and consistency.
- **Data Lineage** – Map of how data flows and transforms across systems.

Collibra Concepts

- **Collibra** – A data intelligence platform for governance, cataloging, and stewardship.
- **Asset** – Core object in Collibra (data element, report, glossary term, policy, etc.).

- **Community** – High-level grouping of governance assets (e.g., Finance).
- **Domain** – Subdivision within a community grouping related assets.
- **Workflow** – Automated process in Collibra (approvals, certifications, onboarding).
- **Operating Model** – Structure of roles, responsibilities, and workflows in governance.

IT & Data Management

- **Metadata** – "Data about data," such as definitions, lineage, and formats.
- **ETL (Extract, Transform, Load)** – Process of moving and preparing data from source systems to a target.
- **API (Application Programming Interface)** – Rules for software systems to exchange data.
- **Data Catalog** – Organized inventory of available data assets enriched with metadata.
- **Schema** – Structure of a database (tables, fields, relationships).
- **Snowflake** – A popular cloud-based data warehouse often integrated with Collibra.

Agile Delivery

- **Agile** – Iterative delivery approach using short, incremental sprints.
- **Sprint** – A 2–3 week time-boxed iteration delivering defined outcomes.
- **User Story** – Requirement format: *As a [role], I want [something], so that [benefit].*

- **Acceptance Criteria** – Specific conditions that define when a story is complete.
- **Backlog** – Prioritized list of work items for agile delivery.
- **Product Owner** – Role prioritizing backlog items to deliver business value.
- **Scrum Master** – Facilitator ensuring agile process is followed.

Regulatory & Compliance

- **Basel / BCBS 239** – Global banking regulations requiring strong data governance and risk reporting.
- **GDPR (General Data Protection Regulation)** – EU law on data privacy and protection.
- **HIPAA** – U.S. regulation on privacy and security of healthcare information.
- **SOX (Sarbanes–Oxley Act)** – U.S. law ensuring transparency in financial reporting.
- **KYC (Know Your Customer)** – Compliance requirement to verify customer identity.
- **AML (Anti-Money Laundering)** – Laws to prevent illegal money flows.

Contents

INTRODUCTION

The Practical Guide to Collibra: Building Active Data Governance Programs That Work

Every great adventure starts with a common vision. This book is the result of such a journey — a journey my wife Huma and I have been sharing during long years as professionals, but also as life partners. As the world's only married Collibra Ranger couple, our journey is about collaboration as much as it is governance and technology. For years, our journey was even chronicled on Collibra's website itself — a testament to the fact that passion, partnership and purpose can revolutionize not just careers, but entire industries.

Collibra has been not just a platform for us, but since the very first day it's been something more: a change agent. From manufacturing and retail to banking, insurance, healthcare, pharma, legal and even some Federal Clients. I've had the good fortune to lead Collibra implementations of data from a passive byproduct into a strategic business asset. My wife has done no less, particularly when it comes to banking and medical sectors. Her vision and relentlessness motivate me daily to raise the bar on anything that can be achieved with data governance. She is, by all accounts, my greatest collaborator — and the pulsing rhythm of this book.

We intentionally did not write The Practical Guide to Collibra as a textbook, but as a story – built on pragmatic experience, the lessons learned and the hard truths so eagerly earned. This is not simply a manual for implementing Collibra; it's a recipe for designing governance programs that do the right things in an engaged, outcomes-focused way. Whether you're at the start of your data journey or are on the road to evolution, our job is to make Collibra accessible, actionable and highly applicable toward the challenges you have.

This book is also a heartfelt tribute — to the many people who have walked this road with us. To the teachers and collaborators and Collibra community who have pushed us to think differently and push for more. To the countless customers and organizations that placed their trust in us to help them transform their data landscapes. To our families and friends, who selflessly supported us through each late night, setback and success.

Finally, I owe the most to my wife — whose genius, strength and unflagging pursuit of better makes me a better leader, technologist and human being every day.

This is our story. Now it's yours, too — because the future of data governance is for those who dare to make it practical, purposeful and personal.

Welcome to The Practical Guide to Collibra. Let's build something extraordinary.

I timed how long it took a young analyst in one of my workshops to find a definition of the word "customer" last Tuesday. Forty-six minutes. That's how long she spent cobbling together an understanding of a simple term from email threads, outdated spreadsheets, and wild guesses in the hallway. I know what you're thinking: Oh dear, the poor analysts are at it again. And I concede that it is an inconvenience to be an analyst in a large organization. But multiply your mental image of that suffering analyst by each analyst, data scientist, compliance officer, and executive in your agency and you can feel the cost of data chaos buzzing and crackling like one of those balls you can touch at a museum. The painful accurate picture is that businesses do not fail because they lack data; they fail because they cannot trust much of the data they have. You're keeping this book for a reason. If Collibra is a platform you've heard of, it's because you think it's a company expense, a program, maybe a "nice to have" procurement. But in reality, Collibra is the workbench, the rulebook, and even the water cooler of modern data governance. When it's working as it should, people can pull up data in seconds, see a clear path to every KPI, and face audits that are dull—and maybe even hopeful. It can be as streamlined as a glossy journal. My job, my friend, is to guide you away from the first view, and toward the second.

I am not a vendor rep who came to leaflet. I worked in the trenches—leading analytics groups drowning in duplicate tables and competing metrics -- then crossed the aisle to work with global banks, retailers and health care networks to build governance programs that stick. I've implemented more than thirty instances of Collibra over the past decade—each with its own minefields, quirks, and 'oh come on!' moments. The pages that follow is built on that scar tissue as well as those successes. You won't find ads here, but you will find honesty: I'll share the bruises I've picked up along the way, so you can walk the hallway with the lights on.

We'll return to five ideas throughout this book.

1. Governance is a people sport. Collibra is only as strong as the roles, responsibilities, and conversations you wrap around it.
2. The meta model matters. The way you design your assets—the attributes and relationships that describe them—will decide whether your catalog becomes a bustling marketplace or collapses under its own undergrowth.
3. Agile beats big-bang. Small, frequent sprints make an abstract vision real long before interest wanes.

4. Integration is non-negotiable. Metadata locked in a tool is no better than metadata locked in someone's head.
5. Adoption must be earned. Change management, not executive decree, drives real uptake—and what gets measured truly does improve.

Whether you're a chief data officer looking to prove quick wins, a data steward wrestling bloated spreadsheets into usable assets, a solution architect asked to stitch Collibra into a sprawling data lake, or a project manager juggling an impossible calendar, this book is for you. It also speaks to compliance leads, security professionals, and the skeptical analyst who would rather spend less time arguing about definitions and more time showing results in performance reviews. In short, it's practical advice for anyone who touches data — and for anyone who depends on those who do.

What will you get out of the time you put in? You will come away with checklists that you can copy and paste into your own project plan first thing in the morning! You will create a meta model that fuses Collibra best practice with the bizarre reality of your business glossary. You will learn how to write the right kind of homework assignments so that the developers on the other side of the table will nod, not squint. You will avoid the majority of these common configuration pitfalls before they show up in your bug tracker. You will build training that your users actually show up for, dashboards that your executives actually look at, and KPIs that demonstrate the payback on every dollar you spend on licensing. Best of all, you will have the confidence and capability to respond, "Yes, we know where our data is living, we know who owns our data, and we can prove it."

The odyssey starts with basics like why governance is important and then takes a scenic route through architecture as it relates to governance and how Collibra's architecture takes you from principle to practice every day. And from there we evaluate whether your organization is ready, since launching unready is like putting together a piece of furniture without looking at the parts list. We also construct the meta model, set up an operating model, and progress through agile sprints while tracking acceptance criteria to keep the backlog honest. Technical readers can dive into installation, security, and APIs, while business readers can skim those sections and rejoin us for workflows, change management, and KPI dashboards. Finally, we close with a candid look at common missteps and a framework for continuous improvement—so your platform can scale to meet your aspirations.

I won't say the journey is easy. Management, like any cultural shift, can challenge sacred cows and expose truths about quality, ownership, and accountability that are hard to swallow. But I can tell you, as someone who has sat in the war room during a midnight audit, that the payoff is immeasurable: fewer sleepless nights, faster insights, rulings based on reality rather than folklore. And best of all, a workforce that trusts its data enough to think boldly and creatively.

So, when you're ready, turn the page. Bring your questions, your limitations, and yes—your skepticism. I'll bring real stories, a few proven templates, and a roadmap I've used to help dozens of organizations move from data chaos to data confidence. Together, we'll build a Collibra program that works for you. Let's get started.

I

Understanding Collibra And Data Governance Fundamentals

Welcome to the New Era of Data – and Why You and I Need to Talk About Governance

I recall vividly the Tuesday morning when a well-intentioned executive burst into my project room, waving a print-out of a spreadsheet like a white flag. The sheet had three different revenue figures for the same quarter, with each column labeled as coming from "the system of record." Her question was straightforward: "Which one is real?"

That little piece of paper encapsulated years of rampant data sprawl, redundant reporting tools and largely undocumented transformations. It was also the day the company finally took its data governance from abstract ideal to practical execution. If you've squinted at competing numbers during a quarterly review, or taken frantic calls from a mix of auditors as the filing deadline loomed, you know the feeling. Just like data is our most valuable asset, it is also our biggest liability if it is not grounded in a framework that gives it context, lineage and accountability.

You and I will go through the basics of data governance, and how Collibra fits into the equation. By the time we're done, you should be able to tell a colleague, in non-technical words, why data governance is important, what Collibra was designed to solve, and why our architecture enables those solutions. To come back to this book's analogy of the map and the terrain, this chapter really is the map that you are going to want to reference as a point of orientation as we dive into specific implementation steps in the chapters that follow.

What Do We Even Mean by "Data Governance"?

The term initially gained currency in the early 2000s, where it was often used to describe committees producing policy documents no one ever read. Today, the stakes are larger, and the definition is looser. Governance is the framework of rules, processes, and policies that create, maintain, and enforce trust in data–making it secure, discoverable, and usable. If that sounds bureaucratic, it is, but it's also deeply tied to culture, accountability, and even empathy within a department. Governance is necessary because people work with data, make mistakes, have diverse needs, and must adapt to evolving limitations.

Imagine the data moving across your enterprise as trains on a busy railway network. Tracks are pipelines, trains carry different data sets, stations are applications, and passengers are your end users. Without schedules, signals, work crews, and a central operations center, the system would quickly collapse into chaos. Data governance is that command center overseeing the tracks—deciding when trains should run, ensuring routes are safe, and making sure every train arrives at its station on time, intact, with the right passengers. Collibra, to extend the metaphor, is the digital twin of that operations center: a platform designed to codify, orchestrate, and monitor every rule and relationship in a way humans can actually use.

Why Governance Drives Business Outcomes Now More Than Ever

Some years ago, its executives viewed data problems as a cost center IT issue. That framing no longer works. I've attended planning meetings where the CMO is discussing omnichannel personalization, the CFO is worried about revenue leakage from billing discrepancies, and the Chief Risk Officer is monitoring new privacy regulation around the world. All of them depend on reliable, high-quality data to help achieve quarterly goals and keep competitors at bay.

Governance is now about more than just compliance; it is the foundation of every digital activity. If a bank activates an A.I.-powered credit-risk model, bad data is not merely a technical mess-up; it could be millions of dollars in improperly denied loans or regulatory fines. If health care providers use predictive care pathways, poor lineage documentation can compromise patient safety and brand trust.

That's why Collibra refers to itself explicitly as a "Data Intelligence" rather than a governance platform. That is, to relate governance to actual business value: shortening time to insight, speeding cloud migrations, de-risking analytics, and allowing self-service reporting that doesn't suck. The structure, language and features of the platform is all influenced by that business-first ethos.

The Essential Preliminaries for Using Collibra

But before we look inside the platform, let's agree on a couple of building blocks. All governance initiatives are based on data assets, metadata, stewardship, lineage, and quality.

A data asset is any item of data that is valuable enough to warrant the explicit management of that data —tables, reports, machine learning-models, you name it. Metadata is the information that describes those assets: where they reside, who owns them, how often they refresh, and how reliable they are. Stewardship assigns real people—owners, custodians, and experts—to every asset, keeping responsibility transparent. Lineage is the path an asset takes, from source through transformation to target. Quality is measured by the health statistics you track: completeness, accuracy, timeliness, and consistency.

If you already use these terms daily, you might be tempted to skim—but don't. Collibra puts each of these into practice with clearly defined roles, relationships, attributes, and workflows. A common language ensures that when we create an asset type called "Data Set" and assign roles like "Business Steward" and "Technical Steward," those terms carry clear meaning for everyone.

Collibra's History and it's Place in the Tooling Landscape

I first encountered Collibra in 2013, during a data-quality remediation project in the UK with a large utilities company. Its key selling point then was a user-friendly interface where business and technical leaders could agree on definitions and policies. While other solutions focused mainly on back-end cataloging with minimal user interaction, Collibra embraced community, workflow, and crowd-sourced curation.

A decade later, Collibra sits at the cross-section of several categories: data catalog, governance, privacy, lineage, and intelligence. Competitors are everywhere—some specialize in automated technical scanning, others in policy management or observability. What still sets Collibra apart is its emphasis on human interaction and collaboration, built on top of solid metadata management. This isn't a sales pitch; understanding where the platform fits is essential to setting the right expectations.

A Walkthrough of Collibra's Architecture

Think of the platform as a three-layer puzzle. The first is the **physical layer**: databases, processing engines, and microservices running either in Collibra's cloud or your own data center. The second is the **logical layer**: the operating model, meta model, roles, and workflows that shape how users work. The third is the **experiential layer**: dashboards, catalogs, and portals that surface insights to different personas.

Under the hood, Collibra is built on a modular microservices architecture. Services such as the catalog, lineage harvester, workflow engine, and data-quality integrations can scale independently. Metadata is stored in graphs, enabling fast traversal of relationships between assets. When a user asks, "Show me every report using the 'Customer Risk Score' field," Collibra queries the graph to return lineage, steward contacts, and quality metrics—typically within seconds.

On the security side, the platform supports SSO through SAML and OAuth, with fine-grained authorization down to the attribute level. Multi-region deployment options provide sovereignty and resilience—essential for organizations operating in countries with strict data-residency requirements.

The Gateway to Governance: Data Catalog

Ninety percent of companies begin their Collibra journey by loading the catalog. Why? Because the pain of discovery is often the most visceral. I once trained analysts at a global retailer who spent entire afternoons slogging through shared drives to locate the inventory table. For years they had been forced to navigate with paper maps; now they had a searchable, governed catalog—a GPS.

In Collibra's catalog, every asset card merges business metadata—definitions, owners, usage guidelines—with technical metadata like schema, column types, and runtime stats. The catalog updates itself when paired with automated scanners. That shift alone can boost productivity—but it's only the opening act.

More than just Cataloging: Policy, Workflow, and Community

Governance will plateau if you stop at a simple "lean" list. The real magic happens when you weave policies, approvals, and metrics into daily work. For example, imagine your business requires that any data used in external reporting must score above a minimum quality threshold. Collibra can enforce that rule—blocking certification until the data passes required checks, prompting stewards, and recording remediation steps—often without additional middleware development.

Collibra workflows are built on BPMN standards, allowing you to model real-world processes—such as commissioning a new data source or retiring an outdated report—as automated tasks with human approvals. The result is institutional memory embedded in the tool, resilient to turnover and organizational growing pains.

Real-World Accountability in a Role-Based Approach

One of the most common complaints I hear is that governance feels like "more work." Collibra counters this perception by ensuring that every action is tied to named roles with clear accountabilities. Owners authorize changes, stewards refine definitions, custodians maintain technical health, and data consumers rate proficiency. In practice, it works like a social network for data: your profile shows what you steward, which discussions you've joined, and what endorsements you've earned. This kind of social proof motivates participation—because people know their contributions are visible.

In a recent project with a global firm, we introduced gamification: stewards earned digital badges for completing reviews on time and for achieving high consumer satisfaction ratings. Within three months, participation had tripled, and the proportion of unanswered research inquiries was cut in half. Human psychology matters—and Collibra provides the levers to harness it.

Collibra Vocabulary: Domains, Asset Type, Attributes, and Relations

If governance is like a language, the meta model is its grammar. A domain is essentially a folder for assets, letting you group related items—for example, Sales, Finance, or HR. Within a domain, you define asset types such as Table, Report, Glossary Term, or Data Quality Rule. Each asset type has attributes—text fields, dates, reference links—and relations that connect assets to one another.

For instance, a Table asset might be linked to a Business Term by "implements," to a Quality Rule by "monitored by," and to an Owner by "has steward." The power of graph models is that you can explore these relationships in either direction. Want to see all regulations that apply to tables containing "Net Revenue"? The system can respond in near real time, even with millions of nodes.

Getting the meta model right is perhaps the single most important design decision you'll make, and this book dedicates an entire chapter to it. For now, remember that Collibra is flexible—it lets you start simple and evolve. In one project, we began with only shallow relationships to avoid overwhelming new stewards; six months later, we had expanded to cover machine-learning feature stores and real-time streams, all without changing the foundation.

From Confusion to Clarity: A Day in the Life of an Analyst

Let's make these concepts real with a story. Imagine Maya, a demand-planning analyst at an apparel company. Before Collibra, a typical Monday looked like this: she logs into Tableau, spots a demand-spike anomaly, and spends half the day chasing it down—digging through SQL queries, Excel exports, and old email chains—until she finally lands on a staging table that no one seems to own. By the time she meets with the merchandising team, all she can say is, "I'll get back to you," because she doesn't trust the numbers.

Now fast forward six months after Collibra's rollout. Maya notices something odd, clicks the "Sales Forecast" dataset in the catalog, and instantly sees its lineage graph. She spots a schema change in an upstream ERP extract. Two more clicks and she opens the related change request, sees it was approved last Thursday by the Supply Chain data owner, and reviews the validation results. The quality score dropped because of the change, and an automated notification has already gone to the steward, who's working on a fix. Maya adds this context to her report—and still has time to breathe before the meeting.

This isn't theory; I've seen it in practice. Collibra removes the detective work with guided navigation, freeing analysts to focus on insights instead of plumbing.

A European bank I worked with faced a looming regulatory deadline (Basel IV, which required transparent risk-weighted asset calculations). Their data environment spanned mainframes, data lakes, and dozens of reporting marts inherited through acquisitions. At first, they viewed Collibra as just another compliance box to check—a cost of doing business.

We began by mapping out critical data elements (CDEs), assigning stewards, and implementing lineage scanners. Along the way, the treasury team realized they could rationalize duplicate feeds and retire two costly vendor solutions. The savings funded further governance-driven automation. Within a year, the bank had cut regulatory report preparation time by as much as 40 percent and reassigned analysts from manual reconciliation to scenario modeling for new product lines.

The lesson is simple: investing in governance tools like Collibra pays off when they expose redundancies and break down silos. The efficiency gains can more than cover the cost of adoption—and in the process, turn regulatory headwinds into strategic advantage.

Collibra and the Cloud: What's New, What Isn't

You might ask whether cloud-native architectures reduce the need for governance. After all, today's data platforms deliver scalable compute, managed services, and even built-in catalogs. In practice, though, the cloud often amplifies governance challenges as users spin up self-service pipelines faster and in greater numbers than ever.

Collibra's Answer: SaaS. With Collibra's cloud offering, there are no manual upgrades, no patches for your operations team, and automatic scaling comes standard—while still providing full-stack visibility. Yet the fundamentals of governance remain unchanged: clear ownership, documented lineage, and enforceable policies. Whether your data lake is on-premises or in Snowflake, you still need a persistent system of record for metadata—one that transcends individual technologies and cycles. Collibra aims to be that layer.

You might be thinking that buying Collibra is the fast track to governance nirvana. But here's the reality: tools are necessary, but not sufficient. I've seen organizations with seven-figure software investments still struggling with broken workflows and disengaged stewards. The platform can surface the problems—but it's people who must solve them, and processes that must evolve.

That's why the rest of this book goes far beyond pushing buttons. We'll cover operating models, agile delivery, change management, and measurable KPIs. Think of Collibra as the scaffolding—you and your teams still need to build the house together.

Mind Prep for the Journey Ahead

Before moving on, pause and carry a few grounding questions with you: What business issues will governance solve? Who has the most to gain—and who stands to lose the most control? How will you know if you've succeeded a year from now? Keep your answers close; we'll return to them when we blueprint your meta model, design sprints, and run change programs.

Think of your Collibra implementation as a living program, not a one-off project. Like continuous improvement in manufacturing or DevOps in software, governance maturity grows through iteration, feedback loops, and—at times—step changes.

The Road Ahead

In the chapters ahead, we'll move from principles to practice. We'll assess your organization's readiness, evaluate its resources, and chart a plan that balances ambition with reality. For now, you have a working mental model to steer your data governance journey: orchestrating roles, rules, and relationships to turn your data into a strategic asset. Collibra helps scale and sustain that orchestration far more effectively.

Keep that perspective—it will anchor every design decision and stakeholder conversation you face in the months ahead.

Chapter 1 Key Terms

Data Governance: A structured framework of roles, policies, and processes that ensure data is accurate, consistent, secure, and used responsibly across the organization.

Collibra: A data-intelligence platform that enables organizations to catalog, govern, and collaborate on data assets.

Metadata: "Data about data"; contextual information describing the content, structure, and usage of datasets.

Data Asset: Any piece of data with recognized business value that requires management and accountability.

Data Steward: A person responsible for maintaining data quality, definitions, and business relevance within a domain.

Data Owner: The accountable executive or manager who has decision rights over a dataset's usage and standards.

Custodian: The technical role ensuring secure storage, backup, and access control of data assets.

Lineage: The documented flow of data from source to destination, including transformations.

Data Quality: A measurement of accuracy, completeness, timeliness, and consistency of data.

Business Glossary: A repository of standardized business terms and their agreed definitions.

Domain: A logical grouping of data assets that share common ownership or purpose.

Workflow: An automated or manual sequence of governance activities such as approvals, certifications, or reviews.

Community: A high-level organizational grouping in Collibra, often aligned with departments like Finance or HR.

Operating Model: The structure of roles, responsibilities, and decision rights governing data activities.

Data Catalog: An organized, searchable inventory of data assets enriched with metadata.

2

PLANNING, PRE-IMPLEMENTATION AND READINESS ASSESSMENT

Picking Up the Thread

In Chapter 1, we set the groundwork: what data governance really is, why it has risen to the boardroom agenda, and how Collibra is designed to turn theory into full-scale, enterprise-wide practice. If Chapter 1 was the architectural blueprint pinned to the wall, this chapter is the site inspection before the first shovelful of earth is turned. We're not yet wiring workflow rules or defining asset types. Instead, we're walking the hallways of the organization—testing what exists, probing what could be, auditing culture, and asking the questions nobody wants to raise in a committee meeting. By the time we reach Chapter 3, you'll have a clear view of where your organization stands, how much it can realistically tackle in the first release, and which gaps must be filled before Collibra is deployed.

Why Planning Isn't Optional

I worked with a large global pharmaceutical company caught in a year-end, budget-induced buying spree, purchasing licenses for Collibra. Executives were enthralled, convinced that governance was finally going to be "solved." But the licenses sat dormant for eighteen months because no one had stopped to ask the basics: Did a data stewardship community even exist? Could LDAP serve as a reliable source of truth for users? Had the regulatory affairs team realized their metadata was about to be exposed?

The moral of the story is painfully simple. Collibra can do powerful things, but it cannot rescue an organization from confusion, silos, and wishful thinking. It's the planning and discipline that turn a software purchase into a viable governance program.

The Anatomy of Readiness

Readiness has three intertwined aspects: organizational, process, and technology. Picture them as concentric ripples spreading from a pebble dropped by executive intent. If any ripple fades too soon, the governance effort falters.

Organizational readiness asks whether the culture, sponsorship, and resources are in place. Process readiness examines today's policies, workflows, and decision rights. Technical readiness covers the mechanics: connectivity, authentication, infrastructure, and environmental stability. Let's look more closely at each—while there's still time to prevent future missteps.

Organizational Readiness: Reading the Culture's Thermostat

I always begin readiness assessments with the executive sponsor, not a technical questionnaire. My opening question is simple: "In your own words, why is data governance important to your organization?" The answer reveals everything. If a sponsor talks only about regulatory fears – GDPR fines, CCPA penalties – the effort risks stalling once the compliance pressure fades. If the answer focuses solely on operational efficiency – cutting reconciliation time, eliminating duplicate work – the program may lack the strategic weight to secure funding in lean years. The strongest answers balance risk mitigation with value creation. They signal a sponsor willing to champion long-term investment.

Once sponsors are secured, the focus shifts to the ground level. Is there already a community of data stewards and responsible data practices to build on, or must it be created from scratch? Are middle managers willing to free up their teams for governance work, or will they treat stewardship as a time-consuming, career-limiting distraction? In one insurance carrier, I found teams already documenting lineage in spreadsheets for audits—they were eager for a single central tool. At a retail chain, by contrast, analysts dismissed metadata documentation as "extra paperwork," politely pushing it upward. Two organizations, two very different states of readiness.

Organizational readiness, then, is less about whether governance will happen and more about how energy flows. Place early-adopter use cases where passion is strongest. Where apathy reigns, invest in targeted change-management campaigns. The map you draw here becomes the compass for your entire rollout.

Readiness of the Process: Stage of Governance Mechanics

Process is often the most overlooked step in preparing for governance, yet it's already happening in your organization. Even if informal, undocumented, or inconsistently enforced, processes exist. Someone decides when to retire transactional data. Someone approves schema changes. Someone resolves conflicting definitions. The task before implementation is to surface these hidden practices, untangle their interconnections, and identify pain points.

I often run workshops that trace "a day in the life" of a data element. For example: when a new attribute is proposed for the customer table, who approves it? Who defends the definition when marketing wants to reuse it in a segmentation model? Who mediates between the privacy officer and data scientists when deciding whether masking should happen at the transformation layer or in downstream analytics? Walking through the full end-to-end story exposes process debt—missing approval evidence, redundant reviews, or manual steps ripe for automation.

The output of process readiness is a portfolio of candidate workflows that Collibra can support or automate. At this stage you don't need BPMN diagrams—you just need narrative clarity. By Chapter 10, that clarity will be joined with Collibra's workflow engine. For now, you're building a backlog of future sprints.

Technical Readiness: Infrastructure Without Illusions

Many planners start with technical readiness, because servers and networks feel more tangible than culture or process. But this confidence can be misleading. Collibra's footprint looks simple—one application tier, one database tier, a few integration points—yet bringing it into a diverse data environment is far more complex than spinning up a VM.

Begin with identity management. Will Collibra integrate with Azure Active Directory, Okta, or an aging on-prem LDAP tree? Have your governance roles already been mapped to groups, or will you spend weeks untangling nested permissions? Next, examine network segmentation. Collibra users connect through desktop browsers, workflow engines call APIs across zones, and ingestion services may reach into distant cloud warehouses. Firewalls can be your quiet ally or your invisible adversary.

Storage and database planning must anticipate more than today's metadata volumes. Imagine a new Hadoop cluster feeding lineage into the repository—suddenly a million objects arrive. Will your infrastructure scale without a frantic weekend scramble for capacity? And what about resilience? Your backup plan should align with enterprise recovery objectives. One telco discovered too late that Collibra's SLA allowed a seven-day recovery window, while the rest of the enterprise required four hours—a gap that caused audit nightmares.

Finally, assess integration readiness. Collibra doesn't operate in isolation; it works alongside ETL tools, BI platforms, data quality engines, and ticketing systems. Review API rate limits, connector availability, and in-house development skills. Weakness in any of these areas will slow delivery and lengthen future sprints.

The Governance Maturity Baseline

There are many governance maturity models, but I favor Collibra's because it uses a capability-based language that maps directly to platform features. The model defines five levels—**initial, repeatable, defined, managed, and optimizing**—which closely mirror the classic CMMI framework many executives already know. When assessing, I ask each team to provide concrete examples that prove whether they meet the criteria at each level.

At the **initial stage**, governance is ad hoc and hero-driven: an analyst keeps a personal data dictionary on a shared drive, or a compliance officer tracks retention schedules manually. At the **repeatable stage**, isolated teams develop their own governance pockets—finance builds a glossary, marketing another. Here, Collibra's value is clear: unify, standardize, and eliminate duplication.

The **defined stage** introduces formal roles and documentation, though technical support may still be thin. This is often the sweet spot for a first release—demand is high, but legacy complexity is low. At the **managed stage**, metrics take hold: SLAs for metadata freshness, KPIs for catalog coverage, regular stewardship reviews. Finally, at the **optimizing stage**, governance is embedded in delivery pipelines—new assets enter pre-classified, pre-cataloged, and with lineage already mapped.

Resist the urge to inflate scores for political comfort. Humility at the baseline pays dividends later. Overselling governance as a silver bullet that leaps instantly to "optimized" maturity only sets the stage for disappointment when the inevitable friction of change appears. Far better to be candid about your current level, and frame the journey as a deliberate climb—rung by rung.

Constructing the Business Case: Dollars, Risk, and Strategic Leverage

Once funding is secured, the business case formalizes the rationale and protects your program during lean budget cycles. I usually frame the story around three pillars: risk mitigation, cost reduction, and strategic enablement.

Risk mitigation captures the potential for regulatory penalties, reputational damage, and operational downtime. One European bank I advised had already paid fines for submitting erroneous data. By demonstrating how Collibra could enforce clear ownership and traceability, we built a business case that paid for itself many times over in avoided penalties.

Cost reduction is best illustrated through time-and-motion studies. How long do analysts spend today finding the definitive definition of “customer churn”? How many hours are wasted duplicating reports each month? Converting those inefficiencies into labor costs translates frustration into the financial language that CFOs respect.

Strategic enablement is the most powerful—but hardest to quantify. It covers faster product launches, adoption of AI, and better use of data to enhance customer experience. Framed this way, governance moves from overhead to growth engine. One retail client, for example, linked data lineage in Collibra to faster experimentation in recommendation algorithms, connecting governance directly to revenue impact.

Funding The Program: People, Time, And Money

Early in my career, I believed the right technology could compensate for understaffing. Experience proved otherwise. A Collibra implementation is highly people-intensive, especially at the start. You need a product owner to set priorities, data stewards to refine content, system administrators to manage environments, and integration engineers to bridge gaps. And don't confuse part-time availability with full-time dedication; governance competes with business operations, and context-switching kills effectiveness.

Time commitments follow a familiar arc: discovery, design, configuration sprints, user acceptance testing, and production deployment. Compressed timelines may serve external deadlines—such as an upcoming audit—but beware the hidden costs. Skipping discovery only creates technical debt later. One insurance client rushed through a two-sprint proof of concept to satisfy executives eager for quick wins, only to spend six more sprints reworking missed requirements. Patience early often accelerates outcomes later.

Budgets should cover more than licenses and infrastructure; they must also fund training and follow-up support. Protect at least a two-year operating runway, not just a one-time implementation grant. Governance maturity doesn't plateau at go-live; it expands as new data domains come on board. Financing models must reflect that reality, rather than assuming implementation is the end of the journey.

The Secret Force of the Corporate Change Machine

Organizations rarely practice data governance in isolation. Employees are already navigating mergers, ERP upgrades, cloud migrations, and digital transformation programs. Change fatigue is real — and if ignored, it can stall your Collibra effort before it starts. The antidote is transparency and empathy. In readiness workshops, invite participants to share their current workload and change burdens. Listen without judgment. When people feel heard, they are more likely to lean in and collaborate.

Instead of creating new rituals, embed governance into existing change mechanisms. If your company already runs agile ceremonies, align Collibra sprint reviews with those cadences. If executives only tune in during quarterly business reviews, add governance KPIs to that agenda. The less new cognitive load you impose, the greater your chances of sustained adoption.

Crafting the Implementation Roadmap

A strong roadmap balances ambition with realism. I recommend thinking in three horizons:

Horizon One: Deliver immediate, high-visibility wins. Examples include a curated business glossary, lineage for a key regulatory report, or assigning stewardship to the Customer domain.

Horizon Two: Broaden the scope to additional data domains, increase workflow automation, and embed data quality metrics.

Horizon Three: Integrate Collibra into the delivery pipeline so that new data assets are automatically cataloged, classified, and tracked from day one.

Each horizon should have measurable outcomes, not vague aspirations. For example: after Horizon One, 80% of finance data assets might be cataloged, with stewardship SLA compliance reaching 95%. By Horizon Two, all regulatory reporting could have end-to-end lineage traceability. In Horizon Three, every new data model should be registered in Collibra within 24 hours, with classification happening automatically.

Defining clear, time-bound outcomes reduces scope creep and gives stakeholders tangible proof of progress. Without these milestones, governance risks becoming a perpetual "science project"—beloved by architects, but abandoned by CFOs when funding tightens.

Establishing the Governance Charter

A governance charter should be written before a single line of Collibra configuration is implemented. The document defines purpose, scope, principles, roles, and decision-making authority. It does not need to be a work of legalese—brevity beats density. Clearly state the values that underlie governance across the enterprise. Identify the data domains in scope for the first release. Outline the responsibilities of the steering committee and domain councils, and confirm escalation paths for disputes. As challenges inevitably arise, the charter becomes your guiding reference point.

For example, I worked with a manufacturer where two business units were locked in dispute over ownership of the master data for materials—a conflict serious enough to disrupt supply chain operations. Because the governance charter had already defined an arbitration process, a neutral data governance council was able to review the issue and render a decision within a set timeframe. The disagreement was resolved without executive escalation, demonstrating the charter's value as a stabilizing mechanism.

Surfacing the Data Inventory Baseline

Many companies are surprised at how difficult it is to answer what seems like a simple question: How many data assets do we actually have? Configuration Management Databases (CMDBs) may contain system inventories, but they rarely align neatly with data domains. Source-to-target mapping documents may exist in project archives, yet are often outdated. That's why a pre-implementation inventory exercise is essential – it anchors your roadmap in reality.

Begin by identifying trusted sources for each category of data. Then trace the flow downstream through warehouses, marts, and analytics platforms. At the same time, collect business glossaries, even if they are fragmentary or outdated. Partial inventories are still valuable; they highlight gaps and force prioritization. Automated scanners and lineage harvesters can later fill in the blanks. At this stage, aim for progress, not perfection.

Security and Compliance Foundations

Data governance intersects with security on every front. Collibra makes metadata broadly accessible, but even metadata itself—such as classifications or profiling statistics—can be sensitive. That's why readiness assessments should involve security architects and privacy officers from the start. Review how Collibra's role-based access controls map to your existing entitlements, and decide how to handle metadata that contains personal information (e.g., sample values or profiling outputs).

Be explicit about retention policies. Collibra can link to systems subject to regulatory requirements (HIPAA, PCI-DSS, etc.), but you must determine how long metadata exports and sensitive logs should be kept and when they should be purged.

If you skip this alignment, security reviews or penetration testing may halt your rollout by exposing unaddressed gaps. On the other hand, early collaboration with security can turn skeptics into allies. In fact, I've seen security teams become some of Collibra's strongest champions once they realized its lineage and stewardship features could improve incident response.

Communication Strategy: Preparing the Narrative

The success of implementation depends as much on storytelling as on configuration. During the readiness phase, craft a narrative for each key audience. Executives want strategic alignment and risk reduction. Data scientists look for agility and confidence in datasets. Compliance teams prioritize auditability. Tailor your message to these priorities.

Timing also matters. Speak early and often—but make sure your announcements are backed by real progress, so you don't lose credibility. Create demos or staging areas to preview the platform's potential. Share success stories from pilot teams. Build anticipation gradually, instead of surprising users with the platform on launch day.

Early Risk Identification and Mitigation

A well-structured risk register is your best ally. Capture potential blockers such as implementation delays, resource loss, funding restrictions, or resistance to change. For the latter two, be sure to identify causes, effects, and alternative courses of action. Review the register regularly in steering-committee meetings. Transparency builds trust and creates space for innovative solutions. For example, when a critical API integration began failing during a healthcare client's launch, an executive leveraged the open risk register to pause the rollout and reassign a senior integration engineer—averting disaster in time.

Case Study: The Readiness Journey to Acme Bank

Acme Bank, a mid-size retail bank (fictitious, but representative), had just kicked off a Collibra program to reinforce regulatory reporting and open the door for data science.

On the surface, the program looked strong: executive sponsorship was solid, especially from the Chief Data Officer. But stewardship was siloed. In one readiness workshop, the integration lead was stunned to discover three competing glossaries: branch operations had a customer-attributes glossary, risk management had another, and IT maintained a technical glossary so complex it was unusable to business teams. The cultural readout was clear—there was enthusiasm, but alignment was missing.

Process checks uncovered another sore spot: a 45-day, email-driven approval chain for data-model changes. Collaborative workshops re-designed this into a Collibra-enabled workflow with a target turnaround of under 10 days.

Technically, Acme was a hybrid-cloud shop. Active Directory kept authentication simple, but strict firewalls between on-prem systems and cloud warehouses complicated lineage harvesting. The network team joined the readiness effort and designed proxy patterns to keep metadata flowing securely.

On the maturity continuum, Acme was still developing, with a two-year roadmap to reach a “managed” state. Horizon One focused on the finance glossary, stewardship assignments, and lineage capture for two critical regulatory reports. Horizon Two layered in data-quality checks on customer data and dashboards in Tableau. Horizon Three set the target of automatically cataloging new data-lake objects on arrival.

A governance charter was written early, clarifying stewardship roles and escalation paths. That clarity paid off: when marketing and risk butted heads over the definition of customer churn, the charter defused the fight before it reached the C-suite.

Finally, communication. Monthly town halls and newsletters showcased wins, including one viral story: the finance glossary shaved 40 hours off a board-reporting cycle. Skeptics quickly became champions.

So when Collibra went live, Acme's staff weren't blindsided—they were ready.

Pulling the Threads Together

By now, you've seen readiness from every angle – culture, process, technology, risk, resourcing, and even storytelling. Each of those pieces matter, but they all orbit one core truth: you need to know yourself before you can tell Collibra how to serve you.

Skip the groundwork, and the first sprint won't feel like delivery – it'll feel like a scavenger hunt. And nothing burns credibility faster than promising speed but delivering confusion. Take the time up front, and the payoff is a smoother rollout, a team that's actually bought in, and a program that feels less like a tool install and more like a real shift in how the organization works with data.

Views on the Meta Model

You've now done enough diagnosis to roll up your sleeves and start designing. The next step is the meta model – the skeleton that everything else in governance hangs on. At first glance, it can sound abstract or overly technical, but now that you've mapped out ownership, processes, and tech constraints, it should feel a lot more real.

Think of it like a tailor fitting a suit: the measurements you've just taken in readiness mean the cut won't be generic. It will fit your organization's shape. In Chapter 3, we'll start stitching the fabric together and give this thing form.

Chapter 2 Key Terms

Readiness Assessment: A diagnostic process evaluating an organization's people, processes, and technology before implementation.

Organizational Readiness: The extent to which culture, sponsorship, and resources are prepared to support governance.

Process Readiness: The maturity and clarity of existing workflows and decision-making procedures.

Technical Readiness: The stability and scalability of infrastructure and integrations required for Collibra.

Governance Charter: A foundational document defining the mission, scope, and authority of a governance program.

Business Case: A justification showing the value, cost, and risk reduction achieved through data governance.

Change Management: A set of structured actions that help individuals and teams adopt new processes or tools.

Sprint: A short, time-boxed period in which defined work is completed and reviewed.

Product Owner: The agile role responsible for prioritizing the backlog and maximizing business value.

Backlog: A prioritized list of tasks, requirements, or features awaiting development.

User Story: A short statement describing functionality from the perspective of an end user.

Risk Register: A documented list of potential risks, their impact, and mitigation actions.

Maturity Model: A staged framework used to evaluate and improve governance capability.

3

How To Design Your Core Meta Model

Introduction: From Readiness to Blueprint

In the last chapter, you and I checked whether the organization was actually ready to take on Collibra. We looked at culture, sponsorship, infrastructure, and those pockets of chaos that need calling out before you flip the software switch. Now comes the question: what do we actually give Collibra to manage?

The answer is the **meta model** – the blueprint that tells Collibra what kinds of things exist in your data world, what they look like, and how they connect. When people say "data catalog," "data dictionary," or "business glossary," they're really talking about different reflections of that same underlying meta model.

Chances are, you already have fragments of one lying around – in spreadsheets, in SharePoint, or buried in an old modeling tool. Collibra will happily ingest that information, but it won't magically discover the patterns for you. Without a designed frame, you just end up importing a messy pile of assets with no clear answer to even simple questions like lineage.

I've been called into "rescue mode" on more than a few projects where teams skipped this step because "Collibra has one out of the box." It does – and it's a great starter. But it's generic by design. Collibra can't decide whether revenue sits under Finance or Sales, or if a System should be the parent of a Database or just its peer. Those are judgments only you can make. And making them deliberately is what separates a playbook on paper from a real governance program in action.

In this chapter, we're going to dig into the art and the science of meta-model design. I'll share lessons I've picked up shoulder-to-shoulder with data stewards, architects, and even the occasional skeptical auditor. We'll unpack Collibra's defaults, cut through the fog of buzzwords, stress-test the model with real use cases, and shape a living design that will guide everything you build in later chapters. By the end, I want you to feel confident enough to stand at a whiteboard and sketch a model that can withstand both technical scrutiny and executive questioning.

One common pitfall is confusing an **attribute** with a **relation**. Take "Country" as an example. Is *Currency* an attribute of Country, or is it its own related asset? If your enterprise deals with multi-currency pricing and you need lineage between Currency definitions in Treasury and Finance, then Currency probably deserves to be its own asset type. But if you only care about currency as a single drop-down field, it's simpler to treat it as an attribute. The rule of thumb is reuse: if something is referenced across multiple asset types, it gravitates toward becoming its own asset with defined relations.

Relations – Where the Magic Happens

If asset types and attributes are the skeleton and tissue, relations are the blood vessels carrying life through the model. In Collibra, you can define symmetric relations like *equivalent to*, hierarchical ones like *contains*, and context-rich ones like *implements*. Getting relations right multiplies Collibra's value exponentially.

I like to frame relations in the language of **questions**. What do you expect a business user, steward, or auditor to ask? If the question is *"Which data policies govern Social Security Number?"* then you need a relation between Business Term and Policy. If it's *"Which reports consume data from this table?"* then the relation between Report, Column, and Table matters.

On one pharmaceutical project, we modeled a *derived from* relation between Clinical Study and Data Set. The FDA often asked whether a patient-level data set was derived from the same controlled terminology approved in the protocol. By encoding *derived from*, the client answered audits in minutes instead of days. In that case, relations weren't just metadata—they were compliance accelerators.

Directionality matters, too. *Contains* from Database → Table is not the same as *is contained in* from Table → Database. While Collibra can infer the inverse, modeling the correct **primary direction** makes lineage diagrams clearer and prevents circular logic.

Finally, resist the temptation to invent dozens of bespoke relations when standard ones suffice. Early projects often propose adding *feeds, routes to, stages, masks*—each as a unique relation. That path quickly bloats the model and confuses users. Start with a **concise vocabulary**, test whether it answers real questions, and expand only when you find a genuine gap.

Aligning the Model to Stewardship and Accountability

A meta model is more than an information map; it's a **governance contract**. Every asset type should imply ownership. If a steward can't immediately see whether an asset belongs to them, accountability disappears into thin air. That's why, when designing the model, you and I need to think carefully about stewardship hierarchies.

Take a consumer-products scenario. A "Product" asset almost always lives with the Merchandising Team, while a "Store" belongs to Retail Operations. Now imagine Collibra firing a notification because a data quality rule failed. If the model links correctly, the alert goes straight to the right steward. If that chain is missing, the alert floats around like an orphan email—visible, but no one feels responsible.

One proven way to avoid this is by embedding **domains** into the model. A domain in Collibra acts like a container: it groups related assets and assigns default roles. You might have a Finance domain, a Customer domain, a Reference Data domain—each with its own stewards. Assets inside those domains automatically inherit permissions and workflows, which slashes manual admin overhead.

We'll go much deeper into operating models in the next chapter. But it's worth mentioning here because **domain boundaries shape how you name and group asset types**. Ignore them now, and you'll pay for it later with messy ownership debates and misrouted alerts.

Case Study - FinBank's Consolidated Meta Model

FinBank, a mid-size European bank, embarked on a Collibra program after failing an internal audit around Basel III risk reporting. Their existing "catalog" lived in spreadsheets – eight thousand fields with no relationships between them. The governance office invited me to facilitate a meta-model workshop.

On day one, we printed sample regulatory returns and asked each risk analyst to highlight every field they touched. The colors revealed clusters, which we re-named Core Concepts: Exposure, Counterparty, Collateral, Risk Weight. Each cluster became a candidate asset type. Interestingly, "Collateral" surfaced across three lines of business with different legal nuances. Instead of creating three separate types, we added a sub-type attribute called Jurisdiction — a single definition with room for regional rules.

On day two, the data warehouse team joined. We traced each regulatory field back to source tables and discovered that ninety-two percent of fields came from just eleven tables in the Credit Data Mart. That insight helped us scope the physical model: limit Collibra to those key tables, then link them via relations to the conceptual assets.

By day three, we had a prototype running in Collibra. The model contained fourteen asset types, twenty-six attributes, and nine relations. We loaded a subset of data and ran a lineage report from Basel Report all the way back to Core Banking columns. For the first time, the auditors saw both the semantic link and the physical path in one place — and flagged it as a major improvement over prior reviews.

Eighteen months later, FinBank cleared its Basel III audit. While many factors contributed — new controls, updated reconciliations, and stronger stewardship — the governance office credited the meta model as a key enabler. Queries that once took weeks were being answered in hours. Even better, when FinBank acquired a fintech startup, the model scaled easily: the due-diligence team spun up a new domain for the startup's assets and reused existing relations.

The payoff justified the three intense workshop days many times over.

Iterative Modeling – The Two-Week Rule

Perfection is the enemy of progress. I advocate what I call the Two-Week Rule: if a prototype cannot be sketched, built, and tested within two weeks, it is too ambitious for a first iteration. Collibra's agility allows you to evolve the model without re-writing ingestion pipelines. Start small, validate, and expand.

For instance, begin with only Business Term, Table, and Column asset types plus the relations "defines" and "contains." Load one subject area such as Customer. Show the lineage to stakeholders; if they can answer one meaningful question immediately, you win credibility. Then introduce Report and Policy asset types in sprint two, followed by Data Quality Rule in sprint three. Each increment coincides with user stories and acceptance criteria you will craft in coming chapters.

During an insurance client rollout, we launched with a deceptively tiny model: Claim, Policy, and Payment. The adjusters were thrilled they could locate every system column feeding the Loss Triangle Report. Six months later the model included thirty asset types, but widening it never slowed adoption because each iteration delivered value.

Managing Semantic Consistency Across Silos

If you've ever asked five departments to define "customer," you know the chaos that follows. Large enterprises often harbor multiple definitions for the same term – and a big part of meta-modeling is surfacing those conflicts early.

One practical approach is to create a **"Concept" or "Business Term" asset type** that serves as the canonical parent. Local variants, nicknames, or regional spins can sit underneath as attributes or synonyms. That way, Finance's "active customer" and Marketing's "engaged customer" still have their place, but both connect back to the parent definition everyone can see.

Collibra helps here with a **status attribute** you can set to "deprecated" once harmonization is complete. That means older synonyms don't disappear overnight but get flagged, and workflows can quietly stop new assets from referencing them. It's a subtle control – but it prevents your model from ballooning into a junk drawer of outdated terms.

Technical Lineage - Bridging Conceptual and Physical

Here's where the rubber meets the road. Business sponsors care about meaning – the "what." Architects care about tables, columns, and pipelines – the "where." Your meta model has to keep both camps happy, which means honoring abstraction layers.

A simple trick: **split out logical and physical assets**. For example, you might model a "Product" entity at the logical level, then link it with an "implemented by" relation to the PROD01 table and its PROD01.BRAND column. In Collibra's lineage view, that bridge lets you follow the thread from concept to column without drowning in every intermediate ETL hop.

But beware the flood. Modern scanners can shovel thousands of tables and fields into Collibra overnight. Left unchecked, they turn your clean model into a junkyard. One tactic I use: stage all new technical assets in a **quarantine domain** first. Stewards can then review and decide what belongs in the core model. Automation brings speed – but governance provides judgment.

Extensibility, Versioning, and the Risk of Over-Modeling

Change is inevitable. Companies merge, regulators add new rules, and whole data stacks migrate to the cloud. A solid meta model needs to flex with that reality. Luckily, Collibra lets you **version asset types and relations**. You can sneak in a new attribute as optional, test the waters with an impact analysis, and only later flip the switch to make it mandatory. Think evolution, not revolution.

Now, a word of caution: don't fall into the trap of **over-modeling**. It's surprisingly easy to slip into "ERD mode" and try to model every detail under the sun. But remember – Collibra isn't your warehouse schema tool; it's your **governance fabric**. If a detail doesn't help with governance, leave it out.

I once saw a team go all-in and create separate asset types for "Decimal Column," "Integer Column," and "Date Column." The idea was noble — type checking — but users ignored it, the catalog ballooned to 48 asset types, search slowed to a crawl, and new users ran for the hills. We scrapped it and went back to a single "Column" asset with a **data type attribute**. Clean, simple, and far more usable.

Moral of the story: keep the model lean, and let it breathe. Governance thrives on simplicity.

Visualization and Communication - Whiteboards to Dashboards

Meta-model design succeeds or fails on how well you tell the story. I've used everything from whiteboards to sticky notes to **Lego bricks** to explain asset types. The trick is to meet people where they are.

When I'm in a room with executives, I don't throw phrases like *"many-to-many relation between Report and Business Term."* Their eyes glaze over. Instead, I say something like:

"See this number on your dashboard? It comes from a single definition here. So when Finance updates the definition, your dashboard updates too—no surprises, no inconsistencies."

That's when the lightbulbs go off.

Once the story clicks, we can swap the whiteboard sketches for

Collibra's **Diagram view**. Suddenly, those abstract arrows and boxes turn into something alive—a map of how their world of data really connects. When stakeholders see their own vocabulary reflected back at them in the tool, adoption comes naturally.

Bottom line: the meta model isn't just a backend configuration. It's a **living artifact** people will look at every day. If you make it relatable, they'll trust it—and use it.

Prototyping Inside Collibra – A Hands-On Walkthrough

Here's a moment I'll never forget. I was running a workshop with a utilities company, and we opened up a brand-new Collibra environment together. Everyone was staring at a blank screen, waiting for magic.

So, I clicked into **Settings → Asset Type → Add**, and we created our very first one: **"Meter Reading."** We gave it a couple of attributes: Reading Date, Consumption Amount, Unit of Measure. Then we made another one: **"Meter Device"** with Serial Number and Installation Date.

Next came the fun part: defining the relation. We set it so a Meter Reading was *"sourced from"* a Meter Device. Collibra asked for the inverse, so we chose *"produces."* Suddenly, the pieces started connecting.

We wrapped it up by creating a domain called **Field Operations** and gave stewardship to Alice, ownership to Bob. Then we imported a tiny CSV with just ten sample meter readings. Within seconds, Collibra showed a lineage: *Meter Reading 12345 sourced from Meter Device A-001, owned by Field Operations.*

That's when the room lit up. Alice clicked into Meter Reading 12345, attached a Data Quality rule on the spot, and everyone could see how their field data actually tied back to billing accuracy. From a blank slate to a working prototype in under an hour—and you could feel the excitement buzzing around the table.

Testing and Validation - Breaking the Model on Purpose

Of course, we didn't stop there. Before you pat yourself on the back, you've got to try and break the model on purpose. Ask the tough questions:

- Where does net revenue actually roll up from?
- Who owns the logic for calculated fields?
- Which datasets feed the anti-money laundering algorithms?

When you can't answer in Collibra, that's where your model has gaps.

I saw this firsthand on a healthcare project. We realized "Patient Consent Form" wasn't linked to "Data Sharing Agreement." That missing relation could've spelled trouble. So we added a simple relation– "authorizes." Suddenly, compliance officers could pull up a matrix of consent coverage instantly. That tiny afternoon fix probably saved them millions in fines.

Migrating Legacy Metadata

Almost every company I've worked with starts with a pile of old metadata artifacts – XML exports, ERWin models, Excel sheets, or bits tucked away in integration tools. The instinct? Dump it all into Collibra and sort it out later. My advice: don't.

Instead, treat it like moving house. You don't take every dusty box from the attic straight into the new living room. You sort. You ask: *Does this actually matter?*

One telecom I worked with learned this the hard way. We set up a conversion spreadsheet to map each legacy field into the new meta model. Every time something didn't fit, we stopped and asked why. Within a few days, we realized that nearly a third of their legacy attributes had no real owner, no purpose, no value. They'd just... accumulated.

By discarding them before migration, we made the new environment leaner, faster, and actually useful. The team joked it felt like a spring cleaning for their data. And honestly, that's exactly what it was.

Maintaining the Model - Governance of Governance

Here's the thing nobody likes to hear: once you've built your shiny new meta model, the work doesn't stop. In fact, that's when a new kind of work begins — keeping the thing alive.

Think of it like a garden. If you don't prune, weed, and occasionally replant, it becomes overgrown. Same with your model. Left unchecked, new requests, quick fixes, and "just add this one thing" moments will turn your clean design into spaghetti.

That's why I recommend setting up a regular cadence — maybe once a month — where stewards can propose tweaks. Collibra's workflow engine can make this painless: route a change request to a "Meta Model Council," capture the impact analysis, and log the decision for audit. Now you've got a tidy record of how your garden grows.

One e-commerce company I worked with even used **semantic versioning** for their model, just like software. v1.0 was their launch, v1.1 added an attribute to Product, and v2.0 was a big release with multi-language support. Every update triggered fresh training material, so end users never had to log in Monday morning to find surprise fields sprouting out of nowhere.

The lesson? Treat your meta model like source code — version it, document it, and keep it evolving in a controlled way. It's governance of governance.

Conclusion - Your Blueprint for All That Follows

Designing a meta model isn't just clicking buttons in Collibra. It's anthropology (figuring out how people actually talk about data), engineering (making it technically work), and diplomacy (getting folks to agree when their vocabularies collide). Done well, it becomes the Rosetta Stone that translates business strategy into technical reality.

In this chapter, we've walked through how to harvest real business language, pick asset types, shape attributes, and stitch together relations that actually answer questions people care about. You've seen how a good model can save an audit, speed up analytics, or just make someone's Monday morning a lot less painful.

But the blueprint is only the start. Next, we'll breathe life into it. Chapter 4 takes us into the operating model – the roles, responsibilities, and decision-making rituals that make governance a living system instead of a static diagram. That's when the model you just designed really starts to hum.

Chapter 3 Key Terms

Meta Model: The blueprint describing how data assets, attributes, and relationships are structured in Collibra.

Asset Type: A category of items in Collibra (e.g., Table, Report, Business Term).

Attribute: A property or characteristic of an asset (e.g., data type, owner, description).

Relation: A defined link between assets showing how they connect or depend on each other.

Domain Hierarchy: The layered grouping of communities and domains for organizing assets and permissions.

Stewardship Model: The structure defining who maintains each data asset and how accountability flows.

Semantic Consistency: Agreement on definitions and meaning of terms across teams and systems.

Lineage Bridge: The connection between conceptual business assets and their physical database counterparts.

Versioning: The practice of maintaining controlled updates to the meta model to track evolution.

Over-Modeling: Creating an unnecessarily complex meta model that hinders usability and adoption.

Impact Analysis: An assessment of how a proposed meta model change affects other assets and processes.

4

Establishing Your Governance Operating Model

A gentle handoff from the meta model

In the last chapter, you and I sketched the skeleton of your program. We defined the asset classes, the attributes that matter to your organization, and the relationships that let Collibra describe your data landscape with nuance and precision. That work felt deeply architectural – almost academic. But it's only half the story.

A beautifully designed meta model can die on the vine if no one feels responsible for populating it, curating it, and resolving the inevitable conflicts that pop up when your catalog becomes the single point of truth. The moment we click **Save** on the meta model, our attention has to swing immediately to the living, breathing community that will animate it.

That community needs an operating model – a repeatable,

transparent way of making decisions, assigning accountability, and sustaining momentum.

When I implemented Collibra for a regional bank a few years ago, the technical build took just eight weeks. The operating model work? That swallowed six months of energetic debate, whiteboard sessions, and more than a few late-night pizza deliveries. The bottleneck was never the technology. It was the fundamental question: **"Who gets to decide what?"**

This chapter will help you answer that question for your own organization. Just as importantly, it will show you how to embed those answers directly inside Collibra, so governance doesn't just live in a slide deck — it lives in the tool your users touch every day.

Why a governance operating model matters

At first glance, many stakeholders assume Collibra is the operating model. They see workflow engines, responsibility assignments, and ownership fields and think the platform will magically drive governance. In practice, the opposite is true. Collibra is a mirror. It reflects the clarity — or the confusion — that already exists in the organization. If decision rights are ambiguous, Collibra will simply make that ambiguity more visible through stalled approvals, orphaned assets, and long queues of unresolved data quality issues.

I once worked with a large insurance company that fell into this trap – their shiny new rollout was expected to "self-regulate," but within weeks workflows were backing up, assets had no owners, and analysts grew frustrated waiting for approvals that never came. The technology wasn't the problem; it was the absence of an operating model. When they introduced a simple RACI chart and mapped those roles into Collibra, the change was dramatic: approvals sped up, duplicate reports were retired, and stewards finally had the space to focus on meaningful work.

That's why an explicit operating model is non-negotiable. It delivers three priceless benefits:

1. **It prevents duplication of effort**. Everyone knows who owns what, and when escalation is appropriate.
2. **It accelerates decision-making**. When a data scientist needs access to newly ingested customer sentiment data, they should instantly know which business owner approves usage and which steward ensures the lineage is documented.
3. **It creates psychological safety**. Teams engage more fully when they understand their boundaries, their responsibilities, and when they see that the framework values collaboration over blame.

Core principles that anchor every model

Every company's operating model ends up looking a little

different, shaped by its culture, politics, and appetite for change. But after working with dozens of organizations, I've yet to see a durable model that didn't rest on three non-negotiables.

First: subsidiarity. Decisions should be made as close as possible to the work. If a data engineer wants to tweak a schema in their own domain, they shouldn't have to wait for a monthly steering committee meeting. Push authority downward where the expertise actually lives — that's how you keep momentum alive.

Second: transparency. Nothing breeds distrust faster than hidden approvals or "mystery exceptions." Every waiver, exception, and decision needs to be visible to anyone with a legitimate reason to know. Collibra makes this easier — the history tab becomes a running logbook of decisions, a record that outlives personnel changes or shifting priorities.

Third: adaptability. The one certainty in governance is change — new regulations arrive, organizations reorganize, analytic tools evolve. If your operating model can't flex with those shifts, it will snap under the weight. That's why I encourage teams to treat their governance processes like software: version them, review them regularly, and be willing to adjust. Collibra's workflow versioning helps you evolve without losing the past.

Decision rights: untangling the invisible web

I'll never forget one workshop where I asked a simple question: *"Who can authorize a new customer segment in the marketing mart?"* Four hands shot up, each attached to someone certain they had final say. That moment captured the invisible web that slows down data work in most organizations: decision rights are scattered, fuzzy, and sometimes contradictory.

The first real step in designing your operating model is to **map decision rights**. Think like an investigative journalist. Trace each domain – finance, HR, supply chain – and interview the folks who already approve changes informally. You'll quickly see the patterns: some domains funnel authority to a single VP, while others rely on cross-functional committees. Document those variations; ambiguity is your enemy.

Next, **stress-test your map with scenarios.** Walk through a request: add a new data element, push it to production, deprecate an attribute. At each step, ask, "Who signs off?" If the answer is "it depends," you haven't dug deep enough.

Finally, **embed clarity into Collibra itself.** Communities and domains should each have exactly one accountable business owner. You can spread responsibility across stewards, but accountability has to live in one place. Why? Because when something stalls, you need to know exactly whose phone to ring. That single-point accountability is the difference between escalation and endless email chains.

Roles and responsibilities: the human backbone

Roles are the human backbone of your operating model. Think of them like job descriptions for pieces of governance itself. People come and go, but the role of executive sponsor, steward, or custodian sticks around.

Collibra comes preloaded with roles like data owner, data steward, and data custodian. The temptation is to just click "accept" and move on. Don't. Start with a blank sheet and write your roles in plain language. Imagine you're drafting a note to an intern on their first day:

- **Data Owner** - makes the big policy calls, approves critical metadata changes, and can unlock budget for quality fixes.
- **Data Steward** - manages metadata day to day, keeps lineage tidy, and kicks off remediation when rules fail.
- **Data Custodian** - the technologist who handles storage, backups, and infrastructure.

Once you've written something even a newcomer can follow, translate it into Collibra's role definitions.

From there, roles drive permissions. And here's where it gets serious. You do not want stewards accidentally rewriting lineage, or an entire sales team with the ability to delete reference data. Always test by logging in as each role. One client skipped this, until a quick audit revealed that the entire sales org could nuke customer reference tables with a single click. The color drained from the program manager's face — but thankfully we caught it before disaster struck.

The council structure: governance meets strategy

"Council" is one of those words that sounds grand, but in practice it can mean anything from a weekly Zoom call to a once-a-year PowerPoint festival. In governance, councils earn their keep when they act as escalation and strategy bodies. They aren't supposed to bless every schema tweak. Their job is to settle turf wars, steer policy shifts, and sponsor the big-ticket items.

Most mature setups run two tiers:

- **An enterprise data council** - the umbrella group that handles company-wide policy and funding.
- **Domain councils** - closer to the ground, aligned to business lines like Finance, Marketing, or Risk.

The trick is in the membership. Too senior, and you'll get a table full of VPs who punt decisions back down. Too junior, and no one in the room can actually approve a budget or stop a project. The sweet spot? Senior directors or VPs who know the politics but still have their sleeves rolled up.

Cadence is another balancing act. Councils that meet once a year lose momentum. Councils that meet weekly burn goodwill fast. A monthly rhythm works for most, with emergency sessions only when something's on fire.

One client I worked with had brilliant policy drafts stuck in limbo for months because their council met quarterly. By the time they reconvened, half the context was forgotten and the other half had moved on. We shifted them to a monthly cadence and suddenly their backlog started clearing like magic.

Collibra helps councils cross the last mile by embedding decisions into workflows. Say Risk proposes a new data retention rule: instead of endless email threads, the task routes to the council group. First member to approve closes it, quorum satisfied, history logged. The council isn't just talk anymore – it's execution baked right into the platform.

The stewardship layer: operational glue

If councils set the rules of the game, stewards are the ones actually playing on the field. They're the folks who untangle conflicting definitions, fill in missing lineage, and guide business users who are lost in the catalog. I often describe them as the librarians of a massive digital library – they know exactly where things are shelved and, more importantly, how to help someone find what they need without making them feel dumb for asking.

Choosing stewards is trickier than it sounds. The best ones are usually mid-career analysts who already know the data inside out but don't necessarily have formal authority. Giving them the steward title legitimizes the hours they already spend firefighting data questions – and signals to the business that this is *real* work, not "extra credit." But titles alone aren't enough: if stewardship doesn't show up in compensation plans or performance reviews, it gets dropped the moment project deadlines pile up.

Collibra makes this visible. Its stewardship assignment tables show exactly who covers which domain. And when those tables are public, the guessing game stops. A data scientist clicking into a dataset sees right away who the steward is, and can drop a comment or question straight into Collibra instead of firing off "anyone know?" emails. Over time, those connections turn into a community. I've seen stewards start holding their own informal huddles, swapping quick wins, and even building playbooks to share with new hires. That's when governance stops feeling like a burden and starts looking like professional pride.

Embedding accountability: the RASI framework in action

Most organizations lean on some variation of the RACI model—Responsible, Accountable, Consulted, Informed. Personally, I like to swap the "C" for an "S," making it RASI. Why? Because *Supportive* feels a lot more active than *Consulted.* In governance, you don't just want people on the sidelines giving opinions—you want them rolling up their sleeves and helping the work move forward.

The trick is not to treat RASI like some compliance artifact that gets buried in SharePoint. It should be a living contract. I once ran a workshop at an insurance carrier where we put a giant whiteboard in the middle of the room and walked through common activities: onboarding a new data source, tweaking glossary terms, granting an exception. For each one we asked: Who actually leads this? Who gives the final yes/no? Who's in the trenches supporting? Who just needs to know it happened?

The funny part was watching disagreements surface in real time. More than once, two people raised their hands and said, "Wait, I thought *I* was accountable for that." We didn't rush past it—we stopped, hashed it out, and came to a decision everyone could live with. That two-hour session produced a huge, messy matrix of tasks and roles. But honestly? The alignment we forged in that room was worth more than the spreadsheet we walked away with.

Once you've got your version of the matrix, Collibra is where you make it real. If your operating model says the data owner approves glossary additions, then the workflow should send it to the data owner, not the steward. The moment your process and your platform get out of sync, trust erodes. The real maturity test is whether people see Collibra and say, "Yep, that's exactly how we agreed to work."

Funding and sustainability: money talks

Governance requires sustained investment, yet many programs falter because funding evaporates after the initial launch. Embedding financial accountability into the operating model is therefore critical. The simplest mechanism is a chargeback model where consuming domains pay for steward time proportional to catalog usage. More nuanced variants allocate costs based on data risk scores or regulatory exposure. Whichever scheme you adopt, document it in your operating charter and communicate early. Surprises breed resistance.

In Collibra you can capture funding details as attributes on domains or communities. For instance, each domain might store its allocated governance budget, renewal date, and cost center. Linking budgets to domains allows you to generate dashboards showing how investment correlates with catalog completeness or data quality scores. When the finance committee questions next year's ask, you possess empirical evidence rather than vague narratives.

Operating cadence: rituals that keep the lights on

One of the easiest ways for a governance program to quietly die is... silence. If meetings only happen when there's a fire drill, people forget governance exists until they're angry about it. That's why cadence matters – it keeps the lights on.

In practice, this doesn't mean endless calendar spam. Think of it like a heartbeat:

- Daily check-ins are light — just glancing at dashboards to catch data quality issues before they snowball.
- Weekly huddles are where stewards swap notes and clean up the backlog (yes, even a data catalog has a backlog).
- Monthly councils are when the grown-ups step in to settle disputes and bless policy changes.
- And quarterly reviews? That's the big picture reset — are we actually moving the needle or just keeping busy?

I've seen teams try to "wing it" and it never lasts. People slip back into day jobs, and governance becomes that dusty slide deck no one touches. The trick is to bake the rhythm right into Collibra: auto-reminders, calendar invites, and workflows that nudge the right people at the right time. When the cadence lives in the platform, governance stops feeling like an extracurricular chore and starts feeling like part of how the business runs.

Using Collibra features to reinforce the model

Your operating model should show up everywhere your users interact with data, but Collibra is the hub where it all comes together. Use welcome pages to post charters, council diagrams, and escalation routes so no one has to dig for them. Configure notifications so emails don't just say "task pending," but tell people exactly what to do in their role. Customize asset views so a business user sees "owner, steward, council" right there, instead of hunting for context.

Workflows are the real muscle here. They should reflect *your* process, not the other way around. If the model says data owners get seven days to review requests before the council steps in, bake that timer into the workflow. If stewards need to capture lineage before approval, add that as a checkpoint. Collibra's scripting lets you fine-tune almost anything—so don't be shy about using it.

One client joked that their seven-day review clock was like an egg timer for governance: no one wanted their request to "ding" into escalation. That's the goal—users feel the pull of the operating model without stopping to think about it. Collibra makes the guidance invisible, so people can focus on building value while governance runs in the background.

Cultural considerations and organizational politics

Technical clarity can crumble when confronted by culture. Some regions value hierarchy; others prize consensus. I once worked with a Japanese conglomerate where saving face was paramount. Direct escalation to a council without showing respect to intermediate managers would have been a cultural faux pas. We adapted by inserting optional courtesy approvals that, while not strictly required, honored local customs.

Similarly, mergers and acquisitions introduce power dynamics. Newly acquired teams may distrust central governance, fearing loss of autonomy. Your operating model must balance respect for local nuance with global standards. One effective tactic is establishing federated councils: global standards teams set broad policy, while local councils tailor implementation. Collibra's domain inheritance supports this elegantly. Global policies live at the top domain, cascading down unless explicitly overridden.

Embracing culture does not mean surrendering to entropy. Define non-negotiables—core data policies, security controls—and socialize them relentlessly. Use storytelling to illustrate how the operating model protects reputation and accelerates analytics rather than stifling creativity.

Case study: MidBank's journey from chaos to clarity

MidBank, a mid-size retail bank in the Midwest, embarked on a Collibra implementation after a regulatory audit revealed inconsistent customer data definitions across lending and wealth management divisions. The data office prioritized the meta model but underestimated operating model complexity.

During the first quarter, stewards were "nominated" informally and given no dedicated time. Workflows stalled, and catalog completeness plateaued at thirty percent. I was brought in to diagnose the issue. We started by mapping decision rights and discovered that branch operations retained final say over customer attributes even though lending owned data contracts. Conflicts were frequent and silent, ending in stalemate.

We convened a two-day workshop with senior leadership. On day one, we surfaced every decision conflict on sticky notes. On day two, we assigned single accountable parties and defined an escalation path to a newly formed Data Governance Council chaired by the COO. Stewards were formally assigned, given ten percent of their capacity for governance tasks, and performance goals were adjusted accordingly.

Within three months catalog completeness rose to eighty percent. The bank's regulators praised the clarity of decision rights, and internal morale improved because employees finally knew where to bring questions. The operating model succeeded not because of perfection but because of explicitness. Collibra became the system of record for accountability.

Pitfalls to avoid

Operating models fail in predictable ways. The first pitfall is overcomplication. I once saw a model with twelve layers of approval for a single glossary term. Users rebelled, and the catalog died.

The second pitfall is neglecting incentives. If stewardship is unfunded, volunteers fade away.

The third pitfall is mismatched tooling. Designing a process that Collibra cannot automate breeds manual workarounds that erode trust.

Finally, refusing to revisit the model guarantees obsolescence. Governance is a living discipline.

Recognizing these pitfalls early gives you the chance to calibrate. Conduct quarterly retrospectives, solicit anonymous feedback, and study Collibra usage metrics. High abandonment rates of workflows often signal that steps are unclear or roles misaligned.

Maturing the model: a journey, not an event

Your initial operating model is version one. Expect to iterate. As your data landscape expands into cloud warehouses and streaming platforms, new roles—site reliability engineers, platform product owners—will emerge. Incorporate them intentionally. Decommission old roles when they lose relevance.

Maturity also involves democratization. Early on you may centralize decision making for control. Over time, push ownership into domains closer to the data. Collibra supports delegation of administration, allowing domain stewards to maintain their own reference data or workflows. This decentralization increases agility without sacrificing oversight.

Metrics contextualize maturity. Track cycle time for metadata approvals, ratio of owned to orphaned assets, and percentage of policies with assigned custodians. Improvements in these numbers validate that the operating model is not only documented but effective.

A look ahead: from model to momentum

By now you have shaped the human architecture that will animate Collibra. In the next chapter we will translate that architecture into an agile delivery plan. We will discuss sprint cadences, backlog grooming, and velocity tracking so that your operating model does not remain theoretical but drives a paced, iterative implementation. Together we will move from governance theory to execution rhythm, ensuring that every two weeks your Collibra environment grows in value, accuracy, and adoption

Chapter 4 Key Terms

Operating Model: The structure that defines governance roles, responsibilities, and decision rights.

RACI Matrix: A chart assigning who is Responsible, Accountable, Consulted, and Informed for each activity.

Subsidiarity: The principle of delegating decision-making authority to the lowest competent level.

Transparency: Open visibility of decisions, exceptions, and governance activities across teams.

Adaptability: The ability of governance processes to evolve with organizational or regulatory change.

Decision Rights: Explicit rules defining who can approve, modify, or reject data-related actions.

Escalation Path: A defined route for resolving disputes or approvals when ownership is unclear.

Community Council: A group overseeing data governance within a business area or domain.

Accountability Model: A framework clarifying how ownership and stewardship are distributed.

5

Sprint Planning And Agile Implementation Approach

Introduction: Bridging Design and Delivery

In the previous chapter you and I sketched out your governance operating model. We assigned owners, clarified stewardship responsibilities, and agreed on how decisions would be made. All of that work was essential, yet none of it becomes real until we put our hands on the keyboard and convert those ideas into Collibra assets, workflows, and integrations. The moment you finish approving the operating model, a familiar question surfaces: how do we actually get all of this built without the project collapsing under its own weight?

That is exactly where an agile implementation approach comes in. Agile is not a buzzword here; it is a survival tactic. Collibra deployments regularly span multiple data sources, dozens of stakeholder groups, and an ever-evolving set of priorities. A traditional waterfall plan that claims to know every dependency on day one simply cannot keep up with the pace of discovery you are about to experience. Instead, we will take the meta model and operating model you already defined and flow them through a series of short, time-boxed sprints. Each sprint delivers a slice of working governance capability. At the end of every two or three weeks you will see real data assets in Collibra, real stewardship workflows running, and real reports that executives can review.

This chapter is designed to walk you through that journey in practical detail. We will start by grounding ourselves in the agile mindset, then translate governance goals into epics, stories, and acceptance criteria that make sense to non-technical stakeholders. From there we will dive into backlog creation, estimation, sprint cadence, and the daily rituals that keep the team aligned. You will also see how to handle common hurdles such as cross-team dependencies, technical debt, and last-minute priority switches. By the end you should feel confident that you can lead a Collibra sprint planning session tomorrow morning and walk out with a solid plan the whole room believes in.

The Agile Mindset in Data Governance

When many people hear the word agile, they picture software developers pushing code. Governance professionals sometimes assume that agile applies only to product development teams, not to stewardship councils or metadata catalog initiatives. I will be blunt:

that assumption is dead wrong. Data governance, especially in the Collibra world, is a product just like any other. The product happens to be a set of curated, trusted data assets and the tooling that supports them. Your consumers are analysts, data scientists, business executives, auditors, and AI model builders. They want to derive insight quickly and safely. If they do not like the experience, they will shop elsewhere by building shadow spreadsheets and rogue data marts.

The agile mindset insists that you deliver value early, measure feedback honestly, and adapt your plan continuously. A perfect three-year governance roadmap that delivers no tangible capability until month thirty-six will lose its audience long before the finish line. Instead, you should expose your first catalog domain, publish your initial data dictionary, or automate your first certification workflow in the first or second sprint. Then you refine, extend, and harden based on what you learn.

Adopting this mindset means relinquishing the illusion of certainty. You admit that you do not know everything up front, and you create mechanisms to discover the unknowns without jeopardizing progress. Sprint reviews, retrospectives, and backlog grooming become instruments of discovery as much as project management checkpoints. At the same time, agile is not an excuse for chaos. It imposes discipline through time boxes, definition of done, and clear roles such as product owner and scrum master. Governance thrives on that balance between flexibility and rigor.

Translating Governance Goals into Agile Epics

Before your first planning session, capture the high-level objectives you defined during operating model design and phrase them as epics. An epic is a container that groups multiple user stories under a common theme. For example, "Onboard the Enterprise Data Warehouse to Collibra" can be an epic. Inside that epic you might have stories for ingesting schema metadata, classifying sensitive fields, assigning data owners, and publishing lineage diagrams.

Why bother with this extra layer? Because epics give executives a view that resonates with their language. A senior vice president may not care about the detailed configuration of resource permissions, but they certainly care about seeing the enterprise warehouse under governance. Epics serve as funding units, communication anchors, and milestones that everyone can rally around.

There is a temptation to create epics that are too broad. Something like "Implement Data Governance" is so vague that it offers no guidance for sequencing or scope control. Keep your epics bounded to a deliverable that could realistically complete in, say, six to twelve weeks in most agile practices if the entire team focused only on that epic. Treat them as practical chapters in the larger governance novel you are writing.

Setting Up the Collibra Backlog

Once epics are established, break them down into user stories. You saw in Chapter 6 how to write stories and acceptance criteria, so here we connect that craft to the planning rhythm. Picture a digital backlog in a tool like Jira, Azure Boards, or even Collibra's own Governance Center if you prefer. Each user story describes a single increment of value that a persona can test. For instance: *"As a Data Steward, I want to assign a classification tag to a data element so that compliance reports can be generated."* The acceptance criteria clarify the conditions under which the story is done—such as seeing the tag applied in the asset page and verifying it appears in the compliance dashboard.

Populate the backlog collaboratively. Include stewards, platform engineers, business analysts, and, if possible, a sampling of end users. The more diverse the authorship, the better your chances that the backlog represents real needs rather than wishful thinking from a single team. Encourage contributors to think in terms of vertical slices, meaning each story should traverse user interface, workflow, and integration layers. For example, "Import tables from Snowflake" is not enough if the tables arrive in Collibra but no one can see lineage or quality scores. A vertical slice would cover ingestion, profiling, lineage extraction, and stewardship assignment so that a user can truly understand the data they are evaluating.

Prioritize ruthlessly. Governance programs often drown in their own ambition, crushing teams under hundreds of low-value stories. Rank stories according to the risk they mitigate or the revenue they enable. The product owner—usually the chief data officer or their delegate—carries the responsibility of ordering the backlog. And remember: the order is dynamic. After each sprint review, reorder based on what you've learned.

Defining Sprint Cadence and Velocity

Now we arrive at a practical decision: how long should your sprints be? In most Collibra implementations I coach, two-week sprints hit the sweet spot. They provide enough runway to accomplish meaningful configuration yet are short enough to keep feedback loops tight. Some teams prefer three-week sprints when they have heavy coordination with upstream data engineering groups that move on a slower cycle. Anything longer than three weeks and attention tends to drift, delaying risk discovery.

Velocity is your empirical measure of how much work the team can handle in one sprint. If you assign story points—abstract units of effort—you can track how many points the team completes per sprint. I caution against prematurely chasing velocity targets. Your first three sprints are experiments. The goal is not to hit an arbitrary number but to understand the team's rhythm. Only after a few cycles should you use velocity as a planning aid.

Establish a sprint schedule that respects organizational calendars. Avoid sprint boundaries that coincide with quarter-end financial closes or known production freezes. Nothing derails momentum like a sprint review that half the stakeholders cannot attend because they are preparing for Sarbanes-Oxley audits. Once you publish the cadence, defend it. Collibra implementation already demands flexibility; the calendar should provide stability.

Role of the Product Owner and Scrum Master in Collibra Implementation

Collibra governance projects blur the line between business and technical domains. A strong product owner bridges that gap. This person understands regulatory pressure, business metrics, and data architecture. They translate those forces into backlog items and negotiate scope daily. If your organization lacks someone with both authority and vision, the sprint planning process will stall in endless debates. I have seen brilliant engineers wait weeks for a steward council to decide whether column comments should be mandatory or optional. Empower the product owner to make those calls swiftly.

The scrum master's job is to protect the team from distractions and ensure agile ceremonies run smoothly. In Collibra implementations, the distractions often come disguised as emergency data requests. A marketing director might demand a new catalog of prospect data immediately to meet a campaign deadline. The scrum master helps the product owner evaluate whether that request outranks current sprint goals or belongs in the backlog for a future sprint. They also tackle blockers such as unavailable test environments or delayed network firewall approvals. Without a vigilant scrum master, the team risks slipping back into waterfall patterns—where every shiny object gets attention and nothing actually finishes.

Crafting the Sprint Goal

A sprint goal is a short statement that explains why the sprint matters. For example, "Enable the finance analytics team to discover certified revenue metrics in Collibra." Notice that the goal is not "configure five domains." Configuration is the means, not the end. By framing the goal around user impact, you give every team member a lodestar to guide their daily decisions. When a technical challenge arises, the key question becomes: does solving this challenge advance the sprint goal? If not, it may be deferred.

During sprint planning, always start with the goal before diving into story selection. The product owner proposes a goal based on backlog priorities, and the team then selects stories that collectively fulfill that goal. Be realistic: a sprint goal should be achievable within the time box while still stretching the team. An easy sprint lowers morale almost as quickly as an impossible one.

Estimation Techniques for Governance Work

Estimating Collibra tasks can be deceptively tricky. Many stories involve human behaviors, such as stewardship sign-off, which are harder to predict than code compilation. Two common techniques help: planning poker and reference stories.

In planning poker, team members independently select a point value reflecting their sense of effort and risk, then reveal their cards simultaneously. Differences spark discussion. A data engineer might assign three points to lineage extraction, while a steward rates it eight because of governance committee approval cycles. That disparity surfaces hidden work and leads to a more informed estimate.

Reference stories provide calibration. Identify a completed story everyone remembers well and assign it a baseline point value, say five. When a new story arises, compare whether it is smaller, similar, or larger than the reference. This relative sizing method bypasses the illusion of predicting exact hours. Instead, it captures complexity, risk, and uncertainty in a single number.

Regardless of technique, track actual effort to refine future estimates. If the team consistently overshoots, adjust capacity assumptions. Over time, estimates will converge with reality, giving you confidence when committing to stakeholders.

Preparing for the Sprint Planning Meeting

Effective sprint planning begins before the meeting convenes. The product owner reviews the backlog, checks story readiness, and confirms that acceptance criteria are unambiguous. The scrum master ensures all required participants are invited, including any technical leads whose expertise may be needed. Preparation also involves verifying that test data, environments, and access rights will be available once the sprint starts.

When the meeting opens, start by revisiting the sprint goal as I mentioned earlier. Then pull stories from the top of the backlog one by one, discussing any open questions. Team members break each story into tasks, mapping out configuration steps, code commits, workflow designs, and review checkpoints. Capture these tasks in the sprint board so everyone has visibility. Next the team compares total estimated effort against capacity. Capacity accounts for vacations, corporate holidays, and allocation to other projects. If capacity is exceeded, negotiate with the product owner to drop or split stories. Finally, the team signals commitment. Commitment is not a promise that nothing will go wrong; it is a shared confidence that the plan is attainable given what you know at that moment.

Managing Dependencies and Technical Debt

In data governance work, dependencies lurk everywhere. You might depend on a data engineering squad to finalize a Kafka connector, or on legal counsel to approve classification terminology. Surface these dependencies during sprint planning and agree on mitigation tactics. For external dependencies outside the team's control, consider introducing buffer tasks or explicit risk stories that track waiting time. Escalate early when a dependency threatens the sprint goal.

Technical debt also sneaks in. Quick configuration fixes, like duplicating an attribute rather than refactoring the meta model, save time now but increase maintenance cost later. Allocate explicit capacity for debt remediation. I recommend dedicating a consistent fraction of every sprint, perhaps ten to twenty percent, to refactoring, documentation, and test automation. When leadership asks why progress appears slower, explain that you are safeguarding the scalability and stability of the governance platform. Point to real examples where early debt caused downtime or rework. Executives understand lifecycle cost when you speak their language.

Running the Sprint: Daily Rituals and Collaboration

With planning complete, the sprint begins. Daily stand-ups keep the team aligned. Limit the meeting to fifteen minutes, focusing on what you did yesterday, what you will do today, and any blockers. If deeper discussion is needed, schedule it immediately after with only the relevant subset. This discipline prevents meetings from devouring productive hours.

Collaboration tools are indispensable. A shared channel in Microsoft Teams or Slack allows instant questions and announcements. When a steward cannot find a data domain in the catalog, they should not wait until tomorrow's stand-up to raise the issue. The faster you surface friction, the faster you resolve it.

Pairing is another high-leverage practice, though often overlooked in governance work. Have a data engineer pair with a business analyst on lineage mapping. The engineer navigates technical extraction scripts while the analyst validates business meaning. Mutual learning accelerates future work and reduces hand-off errors.

Mid-sprint checkpoints can be valuable when tasks are highly experimental. For example, if you are attempting to automate data quality score ingestion from an unfamiliar tool, agree on a midpoint demo. Show whatever prototype you have, even if it only populates a single asset. Early eyes catch mismatches before they snowball into bigger issues

Sprint Review: Demonstrating Incremental Value

At the end of the sprint, you host a review with all key stakeholders. This is your moment to prove that governance is not an abstract policy but a tangible capability. Resist the urge to show slides. Instead log into Collibra live. Walk executives through the newly onboarded assets, trigger a workflow, and show how lineage diagrams now link to data quality metrics. Invite a business user to drive the keyboard. When they confirm they can answer a previously time-consuming question in seconds, you win allies who will champion the program.

Stakeholder feedback during the review feeds directly into the backlog. If the finance lead requests an additional certification step before metrics go live, capture that as a new story. The review is not a one-way demonstration; it is a conversation shaping future work.

Sprint Retrospective: Continuous Improvement

After the review, the team holds a retrospective. This ritual is sacred. It is your structured opportunity to inspect and adapt your process. Encourage honest reflection. What helped us achieve the sprint goal? What hindered us? What should we try next time?

Psychological safety is critical. Team members must feel they can talk about mistakes without retribution. Suppose environment instability caused delays. Instead of blaming the DevOps engineer, focus on the systemic issue: perhaps environments lack automated provisioning. Agree on a concrete improvement action, such as creating an infrastructure-as-code pipeline during the next sprint. Track those improvement actions in the backlog just like product work; otherwise they vanish.

Over several retrospectives you will see a pattern. Teams that rigorously apply insights improve dramatically in velocity, quality, and morale. Teams that skip retrospectives or treat them as perfunctory go through the motions and stagnate. The difference often correlates with the long-term success or failure of the Collibra program.

Scaling Agile Beyond the Pilot Team

Most organizations start with a small governance squad focused on a pilot domain. Success breeds demand, and soon you find three or four squads clamoring for Collibra configuration. Scaling agile does not simply mean adding more people. You need coordination mechanisms that preserve autonomy while aligning vision. Frameworks like Scrum of Scrums or the Scaled Agile Framework provide templates, but the essence is consistent: synchronize on cross-team dependencies and shared objectives without micromanaging implementation details.

Create a shared backlog of integration and platform stories that benefit all squads. For example, single sign-on configuration or enterprise taxonomy harmonization. One squad volunteers to own these platform epics on a rotating basis, ensuring that foundational work continues alongside domain-specific cataloging.

Regular alignment meetings among product owners prevent conflicting priorities. If one domain plans to rename a critical business glossary term, other domains must know in advance. Collaborative planning increments, perhaps every quarter, help teams adjust roadmaps in unison.

Case Study: A Financial Institution's Twelve-Week Journey

To illustrate the principles we've covered, let me recount a project I guided at a mid-sized financial institution. The bank had spent two years debating governance policies but had yet to deliver a searchable data catalog. Executive patience wore thin. We formed a cross-functional squad: one product owner from risk management, two data engineers, one Collibra platform admin, a business analyst, and a part-time scrum master from the PMO.

We chose two-week sprints. In sprint one the goal was to ingest metadata from the credit risk data mart and expose it in a Collibra domain accessible to risk analysts. Stories covered JDBC harvesting, steward assignment, and basic search capability. We completed ninety percent of committed points but hit a snag when firewall rules blocked the connector. Rather than extend the sprint, we pivoted to importing via exported CSV files as a temporary solution and logged the firewall fix as technical debt for sprint two.

Sprint two focused on classification tagging and lineage. The classification engine flagged sensitive columns such as Social Security numbers. A lineage script pulled ETL mappings from Informatica. Displaying lineage graphs in Collibra thrilled auditors who previously stitched them manually in PowerPoint. The sprint review attracted new stakeholders from internal audit, who immediately asked for a fraud analytics domain. We captured that request in the backlog and maintained focus on the current epic.

By sprint four we had automated ingestion, hardened firewall configurations, and introduced a steward dashboard showing certification status. Velocity stabilized around forty points. The team's confidence grew, and executives saw tangible risk reduction. At the twelve-week mark, we had onboarded three critical data marts covering forty percent of the bank's risk models. The auditors reported a thirty-five percent reduction in time spent gathering evidence for regulatory exams. That quantitative win unlocked additional funding to scale the program.

Several factors made the project succeed. We anchored each sprint to user-centric goals, empowered a decisive product owner, and protected the backlog from scope creep through disciplined scrum practices. The retrospective process revealed recurring pain points such as environment refresh delays, which we addressed systematically. In short, agile was not a slogan; it was the governing framework that translated strategy into operational reality.

Common Challenges and How to Overcome Them

Even with best practices, you will encounter obstacles. Let's examine a few frequent offenders and how to address them.

One challenge is stakeholder fatigue. Sprint reviews and backlog grooming sessions can feel burdensome to busy executives. Combat this by demonstrating concrete value every time. Show how new capabilities save them time or reduce exposure. When stakeholders visibly benefit, attendance seldom wanes.

Another challenge is incomplete acceptance criteria. If criteria are vague, stories spill over sprint after sprint. Invest time upfront in clarity. Involve whoever will sign off on the story and ask them to articulate what success looks like in verifiable terms.

A third hurdle is integration instability. Collibra hardly lives in isolation; connectors to data sources, BI tools, and quality platforms must align. Adopt continuous integration practices. Automate connector testing so that schema changes trigger alerts before they reach production. If you rely on manual verification, you will chase bugs rather than innovate.

Finally, watch out for team burnout. Governance work often involves repetitive configuration tasks. Rotate roles, celebrate achievements, and ensure sustainable pace. A burned-out team cannot deliver governance excellence.

Conclusion: From Theory to Rhythm

Sprint planning and agile execution bring order to the inherent complexity of Collibra implementation. By embracing short iterations, clear roles, and disciplined ceremonies, you convert lofty governance aspirations into incremental wins that stakeholders can touch and trust. The process may feel unfamiliar at first, especially for organizations accustomed to heavyweight project plans. Yet as you settle into a predictable rhythm, you will wonder how governance programs ever operated without it.

In the next chapter we will explore how to craft user stories and acceptance criteria with surgical precision, ensuring that every backlog item you plan carries a clear definition of success. As you read, remember that the power of agile lies not in ceremonies alone but in the shared commitment to deliver value continuously. Sprint by sprint, story by story, you will build an active data governance program that not only works but endures.

Chapter 5 Key Terms

Agile Methodology: An iterative approach emphasizing collaboration, adaptability, and incremental delivery.

Scrum: A popular agile framework structured around sprints, roles, and ceremonies.

Sprint Planning: A meeting where the team defines goals and backlog items for the next sprint.

Daily Stand-Up: A short daily meeting for team members to share progress and blockers.

Sprint Review: A session to demonstrate completed work to stakeholders.

Retrospective: A meeting to reflect on what went well and what can be improved for the next sprint.

Velocity: A measure of how much work a team completes per sprint.

Increment: The usable, tested product outcome delivered at the end of a sprint.

Definition of Done: Agreed criteria determining when a task or story is considered complete.

Kanban: A visual agile technique for tracking work-in-progress and improving flow.

6

Writing Effective User Stories And Acceptance Criteria

Picking up the Conversation

In the previous chapter you and I walked through the rhythm of agile delivery, how we transform high-level goals for Collibra into a series of sprints, each one moving us a little closer to a fully functioning governance platform. We talked about velocity, retrospectives, and the importance of a cadence that keeps energy high without burning people out. If sprint planning is the drumbeat of an implementation, user stories are the individual notes that make the melody recognizable. Without well-composed stories, a sprint backlog is nothing more than an unorganized list of intentions. Our mission in this chapter is to turn those intentions into clear, testable, and business-relevant pieces of work that steer Collibra toward real value. When we are done, you will be able to sit down with a data steward, a data engineer, or an executive sponsor and help them translate their needs into language that the delivery team can build, verify, and release with confidence.

Why User Stories Matter So Much in Data Governance

I still remember my very first Collibra engagement. The client was a large financial institution that had spent months producing a requirements document the size of a doorstop. It described more than two hundred discrete features, each written in the traditional "the system shall" format. On the surface it looked exhaustive, yet when we tried to prioritize the list we discovered nobody could tell us which features actually mattered to day-to-day governance. The stewards felt overwhelmed, the architects grew defensive, and the project manager quietly panicked because the Gantt chart was already slipping. We chose to pause, rip the document apart, and rewrite every single requirement as a user story. The exercise forced the team to express needs in the voice of the people who would benefit. Business terms replaced technical jargon, and real-life examples replaced vague statements. The turnaround was astonishing: within two weeks we had a backlog sorted by value, the stewards had regained enthusiasm, and the developers finally understood why they were doing what they were doing. That experience imprinted on me the transformative power of good user stories, and it underlines why you should never treat this chapter as an optional extra.

Deconstructing the Anatomy of a User Story

A classic user story follows the simple structure most agilists can recite in their sleep: As a <persona>, I want <something>, so that <benefit>. Though it reads like an elementary school sentence, the pattern hides a wealth of nuance. Each component plays a specific role in anchoring the story to governance outcomes.

The persona grounds the story in lived reality. In Collibra, the range of personas is wider than in many software projects: we have data owners, data stewards, data consumers, privacy officers, compliance analysts, and platform administrators, each with distinct motivations. A data owner worries about accountability and risk exposure, whereas a consumer focuses on discoverability and trust. When you write "As a data consumer," the words cue everyone in the room to empathize with somebody hunting for information to finish a report before 5 p.m.

The want or action articulates what must be built or configured. For Collibra, that might mean creating a business glossary, onboarding a new data source, or setting up lineage visualization. Resist the urge to cram multiple actions into one story. If a steward wants both a glossary entry and an approval workflow, split them. A surgical cut makes it easier to estimate, build, and test.

The benefit clause is the soul of the story because it exposes why anyone should care. Too many teams skip the why, ending up with

"As a data steward, I want a glossary entry." The sentence is factual yet meaningless in isolation. Add "so that I can standardize terminology across our sales metrics" and suddenly the developer realizes the entry must be visible to the analytics team, the tester knows to check for consistency rules, and the product owner can measure whether the story delivered business value after release.

The INVEST Lens Applied to Collibra

Most agile courses teach the INVEST acronym: Independent, Negotiable, Valuable, Estimable, Small, Testable. In data governance projects the letters take on some Collibra-specific hues.

Independent reminds us to decouple catalog work from workflow design whenever feasible. For example, populating the physical data dictionary for an Oracle warehouse might be done without waiting for policy definitions. Independence reduces entanglements that could stall a sprint.

Negotiable is particularly powerful in governance because policy wording often feels carved in stone. In reality a policy can evolve if we discover better phrasing that serves both compliance and usability. Encouraging negotiation avoids the "signed-off requirements" freeze that kills agility.

Valuable means traceable to data trust. If the story does not enhance discoverability, accountability, protection, or quality, question its existence.

Estimable hinges on the team's grasp of Collibra APIs, lineage harvesting, and workflow customization. When a story feels unestimable, it signals a knowledge gap to address through spikes or prototypes.

Small can be tricky. Configuring a complex certification workflow might swell beyond the sprint if you lump every approval scenario into one story. The solution is to slice the workflow by role or decision point, delivering incremental capability and feedback.

Testable closes the loop with acceptance criteria, which we will unpack shortly.

Crafting Personas that Resonate

Whenever I begin a new implementation, I bring a deck of printed persona cards. Each card shows a photo, name, role, daily frustrations, and success metrics. I hand them to stakeholders and ask, "Which of these people are we helping today?" The exercise moves conversation away from abstract data tables and toward human ambition. You do not need fancy graphics; a name, a line drawing, and a short bio work fine. The point is that when we write "As Priya the Privacy Officer," we picture Priya checking GDPR compliance reports at nine in the morning while sipping lukewarm coffee. The empathy shapes solution design: Priya wants breach notification workflows to be foolproof, automated, and auditable.

One memorable workshop involved a procurement analyst named Frank. Frank had spent years pleading for a clean, authoritative list of supplier IDs. When we composed the story "As Frank, I want to see a single certified supplier record, so that I can compare purchasing across subsidiaries," his eyes lit up. The emotional connection galvanized the team, and the supplier domain became the poster child for governance success.

Turning Ideas Into Stories: The Conversation Cafe

A user story is a placeholder for a conversation, not a contract. I like to schedule what I call a Conversation Cafe before each backlog grooming session. We gather the product owner, a couple of stewards, an engineer, and a tester in a room with a whiteboard. Over coffee and sticky notes, we explore the need in depth. Suppose the high-level epic is "Enable data quality scoring in Collibra." We might tease apart separate stories: one to define quality rules, another to ingest DQ scores from the data warehouse, a third to visualize the scores in dashboards. By the end of the cafe each story has a champion who understands the acceptance criteria intimately.

Conversation fosters shared language. When the steward says, "I need a rule that flags null customer addresses," the engineer clarifies how the DQ tool will profile the source system, and the tester outlines how to verify threshold alerts. The synergy prevents the classic waterfall headache where requirements get hand-offs like a game of telephone, losing fidelity at every step.

Acceptance Criteria: The Contract of Clarity

If the story statement is the headline, acceptance criteria are the fine print. They describe boundaries, edge cases, and performance expectations. You might frame criteria in simple language: "Given I am on the glossary page, when I submit a new term, then the term enters 'Awaiting Approval' status." Behavior Driven Development, or BDD, offers the Given-When-Then syntax that testers and business folks alike can understand. The syntax becomes documentation, test plan, and knowledge base all at once.

In Collibra, acceptance criteria often revolve around data state changes in the repository, user interface behaviors, and integration outcomes. Let me share a real scenario. The story: "As an enterprise data steward, I want to bulk upload business terms from Excel so that I can onboard the finance glossary quickly." The acceptance criteria looked like this. Given a validated Excel template with up to five hundred rows, when I upload the file, then Collibra creates corresponding business terms, links them to the finance community, and flags any duplicate names with a warning. Notice how we specified the row limit, the linkage, and the error handling. Those details guided developers to handle pagination, ensured the steward's community hierarchy was respected, and let testers script validation cases.

I caution teams against vague criteria such as "It should be fast" or "It should be user friendly." Translate speed into measurable benchmarks. "The page should load in under three seconds with broadband connectivity" gives performance engineers a target. For usability, attach a condition like "A novice user should be able to locate the data policy within three clicks from the homepage," which can be tested in a usability session.

Definition of Ready and Definition of Done

The best stories still fail if they enter a sprint half-baked. That is why we agree on a Definition of Ready. For Collibra backlogs, a story is ready when the persona is identified, the benefit is articulated, dependencies are mapped, and acceptance criteria are complete. You might include a quick sanity check that required reference data, such as domains or communities, already exist or will be tackled in the same sprint.

On the flip side, Definition of Done protects against "nearly finished" work sneaking into demos. For a configuration story, done means the change is deployed to the test environment, automated tests pass, documentation in the Collibra Wiki is updated, and the product owner has signed off. I once coached a team that kept closing stories even though lineage diagrams were missing. They argued that lineage was a separate feature, but the user story clearly promised end-to-end visibility. Only when we tightened the Definition of Done did the diagrams appear consistently.

Writing Stories for Different Implementation Layers

A Collibra program runs across three broad layers: core platform configuration, integration, and organizational enablement. Each layer demands its own flavor of stories.

Platform configuration stories focus on objects, attributes, and roles. An example: "As a business domain steward, I want a 'Retention Period' attribute on data sets so that I can drive archiving decisions." Acceptance criteria might state acceptable value ranges, default settings, and visibility rules.

Integration stories revolve around harvesting metadata, syncing with data quality tools, or posting to REST APIs. A typical story could be "As a data engineer, I want nightly lineage ingestion from Informatica into Collibra so that impact analysis is accurate." Criteria would spell out schedule, error handling, and lineage graph depth.

Organizational enablement stories cover training, communication, and policy rollout. You could write "As a sales analyst, I want a Collibra orientation video, so that I can start discovering data without attending a classroom session." While such stories might not involve code, they remain critical backlog items, and their acceptance criteria can address content length, accessibility, and tracking of who has watched the video.

Estimating Stories: T-Shirts, Points, and the Reality of Unknowns

When you first introduce the team to Collibra, estimating can feel like weather forecasting with a blindfold. I have come to rely on a hybrid approach. The team discusses complexity in qualitative terms—extra small to extra-large—using T-shirt sizes. We then map sizes to points based on past sprints. For instance, small equals three points, medium equals five, large equals eight. The mapping evolves as we gather data. What matters is not mathematical precision but consistency.

Be wary of integration stories; they hide more unknowns than configuration stories. I remember underestimating an API story because the source tool's documentation skipped a nuance about OAuth scopes. The team spent two extra days troubleshooting authentication. The lesson is to insert "spike" stories where uncertainty is high. A spike is time-boxed exploration aimed at reducing risk, and its outcome is learning rather than a shippable feature.

From Story to Test Case: Walking the Acceptance Path

Let us shadow a single story through its lifecycle. The story: "As an HR data steward, I want a workflow that automates term approvals, so that definitions become available without manual emails." During grooming we agree on criteria: the steward initiates the request, the HR data owner receives a notification, the owner can approve or reject, the steward is notified, and the term status changes accordingly. Development builds the BPMN workflow in Collibra, deploys it to the QA environment, and hands it to the tester. The tester traces each criterion. She logs in as steward, starts the workflow, logs in as owner, approves, and verifies status changes. All pass except the notification email, which lacks the steward's name. The story remains in progress, dev fixes the email template, and the cycle repeats. Demo day arrives, the steward tests live, and their triumphant smile signals acceptance. The story is done.

The journey illustrates why granular criteria save headaches. Without the email detail we might have shipped a broken notification system and discovered the bug only after end users complained.

Story Mapping: Creating a Governance Narrative

Jeff Patton popularized story mapping as a way to visualize backlog flow. I adapt his technique for Collibra by plotting epics along the top—Glossary, Data Catalog, Lineage, Quality, Policies—and placing user stories beneath in the order a persona would perform them. A vertical line marks sprint boundaries. The map reveals dependencies that backlog lists often hide. For example, lineage visualization depends on successful catalog ingestion, which depends on JDBC connectivity. Seeing the cascade, the team can reorder stories to satisfy prerequisites.

Story mapping also uncovers value gaps. In one workshop we noticed the Policies column lacked stories for privacy data classes. The privacy officer pointed out the omission, and we added stories to classify personal data attributes. The visual conversation prevented a compliance risk from slipping through the cracks.

Linking Stories to Governance Objectives and KPIs

Executives rarely care about user stories; they care about outcomes such as reduced data request cycle time or audit findings. Bridging the gap means linking stories to the KPIs defined in Chapter 13. When you create a story for lineage harvesting, tag it to the "data impact analysis accuracy" KPI. When a sprint closes, update the KPI dashboard to show incremental progress. This traceability silences skeptics who think agile lacks accountability.

I once faced a CFO skeptical about spending on Collibra licenses. By showing him that the story "Enable costing metadata for data sets" directly fed the KPI "cost transparency across data domains," I converted him from critic to sponsor. The CFO began attending demos and advocating for additional datasets to be onboarded.

Bad Smells and How to Fix Them

Story writing is a craft, and certain anti-patterns should trigger alarm bells. Watch for stories that specify solution details instead of needs, like "Create a SQL job to load lineage." Instead, express the need: "As a steward, I want lineage ingested automatically." Let the how emerge during design. Another smell is the endless story, one that rolls over multiple sprints without closure. That often signals the story is too large or lacks clear criteria. Break it down or revisit the definition of done.

I once met a product owner who insisted on a mega story titled "Implement Data Catalog." After three sprints the team still had nothing demoable. We split the behemoth into fifteen smaller stories, each representing a dataset. Suddenly progress became visible, morale rose, and the catalog launched on schedule.

Tools to Capture and Manage Stories

You can write stories on index cards and pin them to a wall, yet most enterprises rely on digital tools like Jira, Azure DevOps, or Rally. Whichever tool you choose, configure it to reflect Collibra vocabulary. Create custom fields for domain, community, asset type, and data owner. Doing so streamlines reporting and avoids confusion. Attach mockups, sample CSV files, or workflow diagrams directly to the story so that documentation travels with the work item.

I encourage linking Jira stories to Collibra issues when appropriate. For instance, if the story addresses a data quality score anomaly, link it to the corresponding issue in Collibra's Data Quality dashboard. The bidirectional traceability helps stewards see when their concerns hit the developer queue, and it helps developers understand the business context behind a ticket.

Coaching Stakeholders to Write Their Own Stories

A governance program thrives when domain experts author stories instead of funneling everything through a central product owner. To get there, you must coach stakeholders patiently. Begin with a short workshop: explain the story format, show before-and-after examples, and practice writing. Then pair a steward with a scrum master during the first few sessions. Celebrate well-written stories publicly. Within a month I usually see stewards posting stories unassisted, and quality improves as they witness the direct link between their words and delivered functionality.

A fun technique involves "story karaoke." Two volunteers read a poorly written story aloud, then the audience rewrites it on the spot, line by line. Laughter ensues, learning sticks, and participants leave with confidence that they too can sing the agile tune.

Handling Compliance Requirements as Stories

Regulated industries struggle to reconcile agile with prescriptive controls. The trick is to treat compliance mandates like any other persona. For example, "As the Sarbanes-Oxley auditor, I want all data lineage changes logged for seven years so that we can reconstruct financial reporting flows during an investigation." Acceptance criteria detail retention policies, storage location, and access restrictions. By embodying the auditor in a persona, you integrate control objectives into the backlog instead of bolting them on after development.

During a healthcare project, the HIPAA privacy officer worried that iterative releases could expose protected health information. We crafted stories explicitly addressing masking rules, audit trails, and role-based access. Each sprint delivered incrementally stronger safeguards, and the privacy officer became a vocal supporter because she saw tangible improvements rather than promises.

Using Examples Instead of Abstract Descriptions

Abstract criteria such as "Proper lineage must be shown" leave room for interpretation. Concrete examples anchor understanding. In a lineage story, include a sample lineage graph screenshot, highlighting how "customer_id" flows from the CRM to the data warehouse to the reporting mart. The screenshot helps developers replicate the scenario and testers compare actual output. Examples also aid stewards in acceptance testing, as they know exactly what to expect.

I keep a repository of example screenshots, CSV templates, and JSON payloads from past projects. When a new story emerges, I search the repository for relevant artifacts, saving time and improving clarity.

The Rhythm of Refinement

Backlog refinement is not a single event; it is a rhythm you cultivate. I recommend a weekly one-hour session where the team looks ahead two sprints. During refinement we clarify stories, break epics, update estimates, and re-prioritize. The session prevents surprises during sprint planning, and it surfaces dependency challenges early. When a new dependency emerges—perhaps a dataset owner is unresponsive—you can take action before it derails a sprint.

In one program we skipped refinement for three weeks because everyone was "too busy." Planning day arrived, and half the stories were unclear or blocked by external dependencies. The team spent four painful hours rewriting stories that could have been refined gradually. Ever since, I treat refinement as sacred.

Dealing with Late-Breaking Requirements

Data governance is dynamic. A new regulation, merger, or system migration can drop unexpected requirements into your lap. When that happens, resist the urge to cram the new work into the current sprint. Instead, write the requirement as a story, size it quickly, and insert it into the backlog relative to existing priorities. If the change is truly urgent—a data breach notification is a prime example—the product owner can decide to swap it into the sprint, but only after ejecting equivalent work to preserve team capacity. Transparency prevents burnout and maintains trust.

Monitoring Story Quality Over Time

A good agile coach measures not just velocity but story health. I track metrics like ratio of stories accepted without rework, average lead time from creation to acceptance, and percentage of stories with all criteria met at first pass. In a mature Collibra program I expect eighty percent of stories to pass acceptance first time. If the rate drops, I examine whether criteria are insufficiently detailed or whether personas lost engagement.

One team experienced a sudden spike in rework. Analysis revealed that the business glossary owner had changed, and the new owner was unaware of existing naming conventions. We organized a quick alignment workshop, updated the glossary guidelines, and rework rates returned to normal. Story metrics served as an early warning system.

A Case Study: From Vision to Value in Eight Sprints

Let me pull everything together with a compressed case study. A retail chain wanted to standardize product attributes across e-commerce and point-of-sale systems. The initial vision statement read, "Enable enterprise-wide product data governance." We decomposed the vision into three epics: Standardize Definitions, Establish Lineage, and Certify Quality Rules. Under each epic we wrote user stories. One such story was "As an e-commerce analyst, I want a certified definition of 'Product Variant' so that reporting aligns with inventory counts." Criteria covered glossary entry creation, stewardship assignment, and review workflow.

Over eight two-week sprints the team delivered sixty-four stories. By linking each story to KPIs such as "variant mismatch rate," the product owner demonstrated a twenty-five percent reduction in mismatches. When leadership saw those numbers, they approved expansion to supplier data. The case illustrates how disciplined story writing and acceptance criteria convert lofty visions into measurable value.

Common Questions I Hear

People often ask whether user stories replace traditional design documents. My answer: stories reduce the need for heavyweight specs but do not eliminate documentation. For complex integrations we still produced sequence diagrams and API contracts. The secret is to attach those artifacts to stories so that they remain connected to user value.

Another question involves writing technical tasks separate from stories. I encourage creating technical tasks as sub-items of user stories. That way task progress rolls up to story completion, preserving the user-centric view.

Wrapping Up and Looking Ahead

You now possess the tools to write user stories that resonate with data stewards, satisfy compliance officers, and energize developers. You can articulate acceptance criteria that leave no ambiguity, forge a shared language among stakeholders, and build a backlog that drives tangible governance outcomes. Operating with well-crafted stories will make sprint planning faster, demos more compelling, and eventually Collibra adoption smoother.

In the next chapter we will shift our attention from the work items themselves to the people executing them. We will examine how to structure teams, define roles, and cultivate engagement so that every story has an owner and every sprint enjoys the right mix of skills. For now, take a moment to reflect on the personas in your organization and imagine turning their unspoken needs into vivid user stories. That imagination is the first step toward sustainable, human-centered data governance.

Chapter 6 Key Terms

User Story: A concise requirement written from an end-user's perspective.

Persona: A realistic representation of a user type who interacts with the system.

Acceptance Criteria: Conditions that must be met for a user story to be accepted as complete.

INVEST Principle: Guidelines ensuring stories are Independent, Negotiable, Valuable, Estimable, Small, and Testable.

Story Splitting: The practice of breaking large stories into smaller, manageable pieces.

Definition of Ready: Criteria ensuring that a story is fully prepared before sprint commitment.

Traceability: The ability to link user stories to requirements, test cases, and business outcomes.

KPI Mapping: Aligning user stories and features to measurable performance indicators.

7

Team Structure And Stakeholder Engagement

Picking Up From User Stories to Human Stories

In the previous chapter we spent a great deal of time polishing user stories and agreeing on the crisp acceptance criteria that will propel your implementation sprints forward. Those stories will sit idle, however, if the people needed to bring them to life are not engaged, aligned, and empowered. I have seen more than one Collibra program stumble because the right experts were never invited to the conversation, or because the organizational chart looked tidy on paper yet bore no resemblance to the way real-world decisions were made. In this chapter we shift our gaze from JIRA boards and backlogs to hallways, Zoom rooms, and lunch-and-learn sessions. We will explore who must be at the table, how their relationships evolve over time, and how you can nurture a culture in which data governance feels less like overhead and more like opportunity. By the time we finish, you will have a clear blueprint for assembling a high-performing Collibra ecosystem and a set of practical techniques for keeping every stakeholder genuinely invested in the journey.

Why Structure Matters More Than Org Charts

When I first began advising clients on Collibra programs, I thought success hinged on getting the technical architecture perfect. Over the years, though, I have watched brilliant designs languish for months simply because no one could decide who owned a glossary term or who had authority to certify a data set. Conversely, I have witnessed projects with modest budgets and sparse toolsets thrive because a passionate governance lead knew exactly whom to text at 7 a.m. when a critical data quality issue surfaced. The lesson is straightforward: governance succeeds or fails on the strength of its human network.

Yet "team structure" does not end with drafting a RACI matrix and distributing it via email. Human dynamics, power hierarchies, and competing incentives are woven into every decision you will make inside Collibra. A data steward can only approve an asset if she trusts that the upstream owner captured metadata accurately. A business analyst will only tag reports if he believes the exercise will save him time on the next regulatory filing. The chief data officer will sing Collibra's praises at the next board meeting only if he sees measurable progress against strategic objectives. Structure, therefore, is less about boxes and arrows and more about forging connective tissue among people who normally live in different parts of the enterprise.

The Core Implementation Nucleus

Every successful Collibra initiative I have observed begins with a small, cross-functional nucleus. Picture the earliest meeting where the product owner, the lead architect, a senior data steward, and an agile coach huddle around a whiteboard. They sketch the first slice of the meta model, argue cheerfully about terminology, and decide which business line will volunteer as the inaugural use case. This nucleus is the engine that converts lofty governance aspirations into tangible backlog items.

You, as the implementation leader, want to keep this nucleus intentionally small because speed and intimacy matter. With fewer than ten people you can schedule stand-ups without poll fatigue, resolve blockers in minutes, and pivot your sprint goals when a new compliance deadline lands on the calendar. That said, the nucleus must still be representative. I once watched a program falter because the technical architect and the governance manager had weekly syncs but never invited a single business consumer. Three months later the catalog looked immaculate in dev, but the business units felt no ownership and refused to migrate assets. Balance is everything: assemble a nucleus that embodies business knowledge, technical depth, governance expertise, and agile discipline.

Expanding Into the Governance Operating Model

The nucleus can deliver a proof of concept, but it cannot shoulder enterprise adoption alone. You will gradually expand outward into a layered operating model. At the strategic apex sits your data governance council or steering committee. In many firms this body reports directly to the executive leadership team, and its primary job is to ensure that Collibra objectives remain aligned with corporate priorities. I still remember the day a council chair told me, "If we treat Collibra as just another IT project we will lose funding the moment a shiny new initiative arrives." Her words captured an important truth: the council exists to embed data governance into the strategic DNA, not to debate column naming conventions.

Below the council we encounter domain working groups. These are clusters of experts who understand the nuances of finance, customer, product, or risk data. They meet biweekly or monthly to review policy drafts, adjudicate conflicting definitions, and approve new workflow steps. While the steering committee secures budget and political cover, the domain groups do the gritty behind-the-scenes labor that makes Collibra valuable day-to-day.

Finally, we arrive at the practitioner community: data stewards, custodians, quality analysts, data engineers, and business users who contribute metadata, raise issues, and close out tasks in Collibra. They are the heartbeat of the program. Your success will hinge on whether this community feels heard, sees rapid feedback loops, and reaps personal value from the platform.

The Delicate Dance Between Business and IT

I have worked with insurance carriers where business analysts owned the data dictionary outright, and with investment banks where every glossary update required a ticket to the enterprise data office. Neither extreme works particularly well. Lean too far toward business ownership and you risk chaotic growth with inconsistent standards. Tilt too far toward IT control and adoption stalls because the business perceives Collibra as an ivory-tower system.

The sweet spot is a partnership model in which the business defines requirements and semantics while IT provides the tooling, integration patterns, and automation muscle. During one engagement at a retail conglomerate, we established a ritual: Wednesday morning design studios. Business product managers would walk into a conference room armed with sticky notes describing desired catalog features. The Collibra engineers would sit across the table with markers and API code snippets. Together they would prototype a new asset view or workflow step in real time. By lunch the group had a viable solution and a shared sense of ownership. That rhythm, repeated week after week, dissolved the usual business-versus-IT tension.

For your program, consider instituting similar co-creation spaces, whether physical or virtual. Encourage stakeholders to step outside their departmental silos, observe how others use data, and help refine the meta model together. The outcome is not only a more resilient catalog but also a network of champions who will advocate for Collibra when budget season arrives.

Geographical and Functional Scaling

Many organizations launching Collibra operate across multiple regions. Time zones, language barriers, and regulatory nuances complicate governance. I once supported a global pharmaceutical firm whose European team insisted on storing personal data lineage because of GDPR, while the North American crew focused on supply-chain transparency. We avoided paralysis by creating regional sub-teams with delegated authority to customize workflows, provided they adhered to a core canonical model.

Functional scaling poses another challenge. Your first wins may emerge in finance, yet marketing or operations soon demand equal attention. The model that scales effectively acknowledges domain maturity differences. Rather than mandate simultaneous adoption, you sequence rollouts so each new domain inherits a stable foundation. That means documenting lessons learned, automating onboarding work where possible, and maintaining a rotating "tiger team" of experts who can parachute into the next business unit.

Securing and Sustaining Executive Sponsorship

I cannot overstate the importance of a visibly committed executive sponsor. The best sponsors do three things. They articulate a simple, resonant narrative about why data governance matters; they unlock funding and remove roadblocks; and they hold teams accountable for measurable impact. If you are still searching for such a sponsor, start by framing Collibra outcomes in language that resonates with the C-suite. A chief risk officer cares about regulatory fines, so emphasize how Collibra can accelerate evidence gathering. A chief operating officer obsesses over process efficiency, so highlight how workflow automation reduces manual reconciliations.

Once your sponsor is on board, schedule regular show-and-tell sessions. Executives are bombarded with competing priorities. Demonstrate progress often. A live demo showcasing how a steward certified a critical data set in under ten minutes can be more persuasive than a fifty-page slide deck. Moreover, involve the sponsor in recognition rituals. When a business unit reaches one hundred certified assets or completes its first lineage diagram, ask the sponsor to send a congratulatory note. Small gestures from senior leaders reinforce cultural change far more effectively than policy memos.

Engaging Data Stewards and Custodians

Data stewards form the frontline defense of your governance program. The danger is that stewardship becomes a thankless, part-time obligation tacked onto an already crowded job description. To avoid this trap, hand stewards tangible authority and celebrate their expertise. At a regional bank we created a "Steward Spotlight" series in which one steward per month shared a five-minute anecdote about how their data set affected customer experience. The storytelling sessions gave stewards visibility, sparked cross-domain curiosity, and positioned governance as a source of pride rather than drudgery.

Training is another critical lever. Rather than inundate new stewards with dense manuals, offer short, role-based learning paths. One method I favor is the "scaffold" approach. We begin with a ninety-minute live session that covers the basics: how to search the catalog, claim an asset, and submit a change request. We follow up with a library of two-minute micro-videos that demonstrate specific tasks, such as adding a reference data set. Finally, we pair each steward with a mentor who shadows their first few approvals and provides feedback. The layered model respects adult learning principles and fosters peer bonds.

Communicating Value Through Stories

Metrics matter, but stories move hearts. When you prepare stakeholder updates, weave in narratives that illustrate business impact. For instance, share how a marketing analyst shaved two weeks off a campaign launch because she found the latest customer segmentation logic in Collibra rather than reconstructing it from scratch. Or describe how a compliance officer generated a regulatory lineage report overnight, staving off a potential fine. These vignettes humanize the platform and counteract the perception that governance is solely about risk mitigation.

During one engagement with a healthcare provider, we began every town hall with a "data minute" in which a frontline employee recounted a scenario where Collibra saved the day. Attendance soared, and within three months the number of voluntary catalog contributions tripled. People crave relatable examples. Give them a steady diet of real-world wins, and watch engagement flourish.

Coping With Resistance and Fatigue

No matter how compelling your narrative, you will encounter skeptics. The most common objections fall into a few predictable categories. Some claim governance slows them down, others argue they already know where to find their data, and a few fear that exposing lineage will reveal past mistakes. Rather than dismiss these concerns, treat them as valuable feedback.

A technique that has served me well is the "listening roadshow." I schedule thirty-minute one-on-one conversations with vocal critics, not to defend the program but to understand their pain points. I ask open questions like, "Can you describe a time governance requirements hindered your project?" The insights gleaned often shape workflow tweaks or new collateral that makes the platform easier to use. More importantly, critics who feel heard often transform into advocates.

Fatigue surfaces during long implementations. The initial excitement of go-live fades, sprints blend together, and progress can stall. Inject bursts of energy by celebrating milestones, rotating team members to spark fresh perspectives, and revisiting the backlog to retire obsolete tasks. A mid-project retrospective, facilitated by an impartial coach, can unearth simmering tensions before they derail momentum.

Incentives, Recognition, and Career Paths

People rarely devote sustained effort to initiatives that do not further their careers. If your organization lacks formal recognition for governance contributions, lobby for change. I have seen companies embed stewardship responsibilities into performance evaluations, allocate dedicated FTE percentages, and even establish data governance badges that appear on internal social platforms. When employees witness peers receiving promotions or public accolades for their Collibra work, skepticism dissipates.

Moreover, articulate a clear career path. Junior analysts who master Collibra workflows should see a trajectory toward senior steward roles, data product management, or even governance leadership positions. Map these pathways explicitly, publicize success stories, and you will attract top talent into the program.

Tooling the Collaboration

Collibra itself offers collaboration features—comment threads, tasks, endorsements—yet you should not rely solely on the platform. Supplement with chat channels, virtual whiteboards, and weekly office hours. At a technology firm I advised, we set up an always-open Zoom "governance lounge" where stewards could drop by to troubleshoot issues. The informal setting fostered camaraderie and allowed quick resolution of minor obstacles that might otherwise linger as ticket queues.

Integration with existing project management tools is equally vital. If your agile squads live inside JIRA or Azure DevOps, ensure Collibra tickets synchronize seamlessly. That way, stakeholders do not juggle multiple to-do lists. Every reduction in friction translates to higher engagement.

Documentation as a Living Product

Documentation is often viewed as a compliance checkbox. Resist that view. Treat your operating model guide, steward handbook, and onboarding slides as living products that evolve through user feedback. Host quarterly "doc jams" where contributors gather to refresh screenshots, prune outdated references, and add new FAQs. When documentation reflects current reality, it becomes a trusted ally rather than a dusty appendix.

Budgeting for Engagement Activities

Stakeholder engagement requires budget—from branded swag that sparks curiosity to professional facilitation for cross-domain workshops. During scoping sessions, earmark funds explicitly for engagement. I once witnessed a program allocate thousands for server upgrades yet balk at purchasing a virtual whiteboard license. The result: brilliant meta model diagrams languished in PowerPoint purgatory. A modest investment in collaboration tooling would have accelerated decision-making tenfold.

Measuring Engagement Health

You cannot manage what you do not measure. While Chapter 13 will delve deeply into KPIs, start capturing simple engagement metrics now. Track active users, steward response times, domain group attendance, and backlog cycle time. Share the metrics openly. Transparency breeds accountability, and accountability fuels continuous improvement.

A Personal Anecdote: Saving a Project With a Single Lunch

Let me close the body of this chapter with a brief story. Several years ago, I joined a Collibra implementation already bogged down. The meta model was sound, APIs were humming, yet adoption flatlined. After some digging, I discovered that two mid-level managers—one from risk, one from engineering—had been at odds for months over ownership of a critical data set. Their feud, though minor on the surface, had paralyzed the entire certification workflow.

I invited both to lunch at a cafe across town, far from corporate distractions. Over sandwiches they realized they shared a mutual admiration for classic jazz. By dessert they had agreed to co-own the asset temporarily and resolved to pilot a joint stewardship model. Within weeks, the backlog cleared and usage metrics soared. The moral is simple: sometimes the most powerful engagement tactic is human connection stripped of agendas and whiteboards. Never underestimate the bonding power of shared interests and a good meal.

Conclusion: From Teams to Ecosystems

Team structure and stakeholder engagement are not static checkboxes; they are dynamic ecosystems that evolve alongside your organization's data ambitions. By anchoring your Collibra program in a small, empowered nucleus and methodically extending outward through councils, domain groups, and practitioner communities, you create resilient scaffolding capable of withstanding leadership turnover, budget shifts, and market turbulence.

Remember that engagement thrives on stories, recognition, and visible executive commitment. Cultivate listening habits, measure participation, and infuse the journey with periodic bursts of celebration. If you do, the people around you will not merely use

Collibra; they will champion it.

In the next chapter we will transition from human dynamics to the nuts and bolts of technology. You will learn how to configure Collibra, establish secure access, and optimize performance so that the vibrant community you have just built can rely on a rock-solid platform. Your teams are ready; now let us make sure the system is, too.

Chapter 7 Key Terms

Stakeholder Engagement: Proactive communication and collaboration with all parties affected by governance.

Stewardship Council: A cross-functional group that coordinates data stewardship efforts.

Data Council: A formal body overseeing data policies and prioritization.

Change Champion: An advocate who drives enthusiasm and adoption among peers.

Engagement Metrics: Measurements such as participation rate or meeting attendance that track involvement.

Recognition Program: A structured way to reward active contributors in governance activities.

Communication Plan: A documented schedule for messaging stakeholders throughout the program.

8

Technical Implementation And Configuration

Introduction: From People to Platforms

In the last chapter you and I spent time assembling the human engine that will power your Collibra initiative. We clarified who sits where, who signs what, and who sounds the alarm when something goes off-track. With that social architecture in place, it is time to turn the lights on, roll up our sleeves, and get Collibra itself running. This chapter walks you through the nuts and bolts of technical implementation and configuration. My aim is to make sure that the very first time a data steward logs in, the platform feels stable, secure, and ready for real work rather than like a half-built sandbox.

When I led my first enterprise deployment, I remember realizing how different "installing software" can be from "making the software useful." The first is a short-lived sprint that involves installers, ports, and service accounts; the second is a marathon in which you coach the technology into harmonizing with your organization's complex identity systems, performance benchmarks, and security controls. In the following pages we will travel that full distance together, starting from the moment you receive Collibra's license key and finishing when your instance can scale to thousands of concurrent catalog searches without breaking a sweat.

Choosing Your Deployment Topology

Every organization carries its own baggage of preferred cloud providers, on-premise data centers, regulatory boundaries, and procurement constraints. Before you run a single installer, you must decide where Collibra will physically live. The vendor offers three principal patterns: fully managed Software-as-a-Service, customer-managed cloud deployment, and classic on-premise installation.

I once consulted for a bank that had spent two years drafting an internal cloud policy only to discover that "internal cloud" did not satisfy regulators who insisted core banking metadata stay inside national borders. Even though the policy allowed AWS, the legal department interpreted the regulation more conservatively. That bank ended up selecting Collibra's on-premise model even though it meant higher operational overhead. Conversely, a biotech startup I worked with jumped at the SaaS option because their two-person infrastructure team could not babysit another production database.

Your choice drives subsequent decisions about integration

endpoints, security architecture, and even staffing. For example, a SaaS tenant offloads patching and routine backups to Collibra, whereas a self-hosted environment leaves you in control of the maintenance windows. Make sure that your governance council signs off on the deployment topology because once the wheels start moving, changing course is far more expensive than choosing correctly at the outset.

Preparing the Foundation: Network, Hardware, and Software Prerequisites

Once you know where Collibra will live, you can turn to the practical reality of firewalls, CPU cores, and JVM heap sizes. Even if you pick SaaS, you must still secure outbound ports, synchronize identity providers, and test latency from on-premise data sources to the Collibra tenant.

During one engagement at a retailer, we overlooked a deceptively small firewall rule that blocked outbound TLS traffic on a nonstandard port used by their LDAP servers. The Collibra application was up, the login page loaded, but the first authentication attempt merely spun until timing out. The fix—a five-minute conversation with network security—arrived after three hours of frantic log analysis. That vignette taught me to triple-check every port and protocol specified in the installation guide.

Hardware sizing becomes critical for customer-managed

installations. Collibra publishes guidelines based on catalog size, number of workflows, and concurrent users, but these are averages. If your business will eventually ingest hundreds of millions of technical assets—think lineage from a massive lakehouse—shoot above the recommended floor. It is far easier to throttle unused CPUs later than to expand a node under executive pressure because the catalog search is crawling.

Software prerequisites are straightforward: a supported Java runtime, an application server such as Tomcat or Jetty, a relational database for the repository—usually PostgreSQL or Oracle—and an operating system hardened by your cybersecurity playbook. What catches many teams off guard is the version compatibility matrix. A classic case involved a client running an older database patch set that missed a minor security update. Collibra's installer dutifully validated the version, detected the mismatch, and aborted. Two weeks passed before the DBA group could complete a maintenance window. Had we reviewed the matrix earlier, the project would not have lost that sprint.

Installation Step-by-Step: From Bits to a Running Service

The first Collibra installation I ever led started with a false sense of calm. The infrastructure team handed me a pristine VM, the database admin swore connectivity was tested, and someone from security had just emailed a fresh certificate chain. It felt like everything was in place—until we hit a missing JDBC driver that turned a two-hour window into an all-nighter. The lesson stuck with me: installation is less about typing commands and more about managing dependencies, people, and patience.

Think of this phase as your first governance exercise in miniature. You're setting the tone for discipline, documentation, and cross-team collaboration that will echo throughout your program. Follow a deliberate, repeatable process, and document every choice. Your future self (and whoever performs your next upgrade) will thank you.

Step 1: Prepare the Repository

- Run the Collibra database scripts to create schemas, tables, and the initial admin user.
- Verify connectivity from the application tier with a simple JDBC test.
- Store credentials securely—preferably in your enterprise vault—so the team avoids "shared password" syndrome later.

Reflective Note: This is where most new admins learn that database performance tuning is governance by another name. A poorly sized repository today becomes a political crisis when response times lag tomorrow. Take your time here.

Step 2: Deploy the Application

- Drop the binaries into your application server (Tomcat, Jetty, or whichever your architecture dictates).
- Configure environment variables: JDBC URL, mail server, encryption keys, and secret tokens.
- Ensure your configuration aligns with your organization's backup and DR strategy.

Reflective Note: I often tell clients, "If it isn't repeatable, it isn't governance." Script your deployments. A single command that builds and configures Collibra the same way every time is worth a hundred perfectly worded checklists.

Step 3: Start and Validate

- Restart the service and load the welcome screen.
- Check logs for background services—sync engine, indexer, job scheduler—starting cleanly.
- Confirm scheduled jobs (metrics collectors, index tasks) run without warnings.
- Observe JVM heap and thread counts for a few minutes under light use.

Reflective Close: This is the quiet victory moment. When that first login succeeds and the home screen loads without error, resist the urge to celebrate too soon. Invite colleagues to test only after you've reviewed logs and validated performance. Small cracks now are what become production outages later.

Authentication and Authorization: Binding Identity to Governance

When I first rolled out Collibra in a global bank, the question of "who can see what" nearly stalled the program before it began. The IT security team insisted on connecting everything through Active Directory, while business stewards wanted a simpler list of names they could manage inside the platform. Both were right — and both were missing the point. Authentication is a technology problem; authorization is a governance problem.

We eventually found balance by treating identity as an extension of stewardship, not an obstacle to it. Collibra supports all the major protocols — LDAP, Active Directory, SAML, OAuth — but those are just pipes. The real design work lies in how you structure roles and entitlements to mirror the operating model you defined earlier in the book.

Designing with Roles, Not Just Groups

Start by defining governance roles that mean something to your business — Data Steward, Data Owner, Glossary Author, Domain Lead. Then, map those roles to your enterprise directory groups instead of reusing generic ones like All Staff or IT Department.
In one project, we made the mistake of inheriting entire department

groups from Active Directory. Within a week, hundreds of analysts could edit glossary terms meant to be read-only. We fixed it by creating governance-specific security groups, naming them by function rather than organization, and managing membership automatically through HR data feeds.

Least Privilege as a Living Rule

It's tempting to overgrant permissions in the name of speed, but the moment you do, your catalog stops being a source of truth and becomes a playground of accidental edits. Implement least privilege from the start – but expect to revisit it. People change roles, contractors rotate in and out, mergers add new domains. Automate deprovisioning so a user's rights vanish the same day they leave. A single lingering admin account can undo months of careful configuration.

Testing What People Can't See

During user acceptance testing, don't just check what users can access – check what they can't. Contractors, external partners, or short-term interns often inherit permissions from nested groups that nobody remembers creating. One of my favorite tests is to ask, "If this person left tomorrow, what would still be visible?" If the answer isn't "nothing," you have work to do.

Reflective Note: Collibra's flexibility is both its blessing and its trap. The same role model that lets a steward in Tokyo manage a regional glossary can also let a misplaced group assignment expose confidential data to the wrong audience. The art is not in setting permissions once but in creating a rhythm of review — a quarterly ritual where IT and governance teams check that access still aligns with policy. Identity, like data itself, drifts if you stop tending it.

Configuring Security: Encryption, Auditing, and Compliance Hooks

A few years ago, I sat in a regulator's conference room explaining why a Collibra environment contained unencrypted audit logs. They weren't production data, just workflow traces, but the look on the auditor's face told me it didn't matter. "If it describes how data moved," she said, "it is data." That moment cemented my view that security in Collibra is not about paranoia — it's about narrative control. Every click, every workflow approval, every definition change tells a story of accountability. Your job is to ensure that story is protected and provable.

Start with Transport and Storage

Security begins where data moves and rests. Enforce HTTPS everywhere and disable weak ciphers at your load balancer. Collibra Cloud handles this for you, but on-premise or hybrid setups need explicit configuration. Redirect port 80 to 443, review your certificate expiry schedules, and test connections with simple curl or OpenSSL commands.

For data at rest, use database encryption — whether native or via your organization's Key Management Service (KMS). Some financial institutions I've worked with even rotate keys quarterly to align with their broader compliance rhythm. It's a small operational cost for immense peace of mind.

Audit and Immutability

Audit logs are your insurance policy. Enable detailed activity logging from day one, and ship those logs into your SIEM (Splunk, QRadar, or equivalent). Don't just store them — read them. Look for anomalies like sudden spikes in failed logins or bulk edits by a single user. In one healthcare client, this practice caught a misconfigured workflow that was overwriting steward comments silently; without log analysis, they'd have lost a month of approvals.

For truly sensitive records — regulatory attestations, certified data definitions, or lineage approvals — consider marking attributes immutable once approved. It prevents quiet edits that erode trust and supports the "four eyes" principle auditors love to see.

Incident Integration: Security as a Workflow

Security should not live outside the governance program. Integrate alerts from Collibra into your incident response channels

— Slack, Teams, PagerDuty, or ServiceNow. A burst of permission errors or failed SSO authentications should create the same urgency as a server outage. When SecOps and Data Governance share dashboards, you stop firefighting separately and start managing risk collectively.

Reflective Note: You can configure encryption and audit settings in an afternoon, but building a culture of security-aware governance takes months. The difference between "compliant" and "trusted" is storytelling: being able to show not just what you protect but why. Collibra, when configured thoughtfully, becomes a living record of integrity — a digital witness to every policy you claim to uphold.

mistakes. Check important info. See Cookie Preferences.

Performance Tuning: Because Latency Kills Enthusiasm

One of the first Collibra rollouts I ever led went perfectly – until the day it didn't. The catalog had doubled overnight after a new integration came online. Searches that once took seconds now spun for fifteen, dashboards froze, and the governance lead fielded the question every admin dreads: "Is this thing down again?" It wasn't down; it was simply slow – and in the user's mind, that's the same thing.

Performance issues rarely start as disasters. They creep in like background noise until they drown out goodwill. The good news is that Collibra's architecture offers multiple levers for keeping speed on **your side — if you monitor early and act methodically.**

Database Optimization

Start with the repository. Slow queries are the silent killers of Collibra performance. Enable query logging and review execution plans for high-latency operations. Add indexes where appropriate, but never modify core schema tables directly — use vendor guidance. Adjust parameters such as work_mem or shared_buffers in PostgreSQL to match actual load rather than default templates.

Run periodic health checks. One client scheduled a nightly vacuum and analyze job that cut query latency by half — invisible to users, but transformative to their experience.

JVM and Application Layer

Your application server (Tomcat, Jetty, or Collibra's container) is the engine room. Use the G1 Garbage Collector for large heaps, track pause times through JMX, and set alerts for memory leaks or runaway threads. In a retail implementation I supported, heap usage climbed slowly every weekend until we realized the indexing service never released file handles. A single configuration tweak to restart the indexer after reindex fixed months of user frustration.

Search Index and Background Jobs

The search index underpins nearly every user interaction. Place it on SSD storage, schedule reindexing during off-hours, and avoid overlapping maintenance windows. Regularly clear stale tasks and review logs for index lag. If users report inconsistent results between searches and filters, your index synchronization timing is the first suspect.

Scaling and Resilience

When in doubt, scale horizontally before vertically. Collibra performs beautifully behind a load balancer when nodes share consistent configuration. Test failover in daylight, not during crisis. A seamless failover earns user trust faster than any performance statistic.

Reflective Note: A fast platform feels invisible – and that's the goal. Nobody thanks you for sub-second searches; they just keep using the system. But every extra second is a seed of doubt about governance itself. The lesson from every slow Collibra I've seen is this: performance is not a technical vanity metric; it's a governance enabler. Because when the catalog lags, trust lags right behind it.

Configuring Core Services: Email, Notifications, and External Integrations

The first time your users "meet" Collibra won't be in the catalog itself – it will be in their inbox. A workflow reminder, an approval notification, or a daily digest will quietly introduce the platform long before most have logged in. That's why configuration of core services deserves more attention than it usually gets.

I still remember a finance client whose first pilot crashed and burned because the default Collibra emails came from an unbranded address. Employees thought the messages were phishing attempts and reported them to IT security. Once we added the company logo and verified SPF/DKIM records, those same emails became trusted signals that data governance had arrived.

Email and Branding Essentials

- Configure a dedicated SMTP relay; never use personal or ad hoc mail servers.
- Set correct SPF and DKIM records to prevent spam filtering.
- Brand your templates: add company logo, sender name, and plain-language subject lines.
- Test delivery across departments – some spam filters behave differently in Finance than in Marketing.

External Integrations

Email is just the beginning. Collibra shines when it plugs into the systems your teams already use.

- Ticketing Systems (ServiceNow, JIRA): Use REST credentials or webhooks to create or update work items automatically. Start with a single, low-risk case (e.g., data quality rule failure → ServiceNow incident). Once stable, expand to stewardship assignments and exception workflows.
- Collaboration Portals (SharePoint, Intranet): Embed search widgets or glossary snippets where users already gather. A manufacturing client exposed Collibra glossary terms on their intranet homepage. Overnight, search queries quadrupled, and the governance team learned which business terms resonated most with employees.
- Monitoring and Load Control: Every integration adds network and compute overhead. Track API utilization and workflow throughput to ensure external traffic doesn't throttle Collibra performance.

Reflective Note: Integration is not a technical luxury – it's cultural adoption in disguise. The more Collibra blends into daily tools, the less it feels like a separate platform and the faster people internalize it as part of their workflow.

Plugin and Extension Management: Balancing Innovation with Stability

One of Collibra's secret weapons is extensibility. You can script, extend, and reshape the platform far beyond its defaults — but with great power comes great responsibility (and a few potential NullPointerExceptions).

During an upgrade at a utilities company, a custom lineage viewer plugin crashed under the new Collibra version. For two hours, users saw blank screens while we hunted the cause. The fix? A single outdated library in the plugin. The lesson? Treat plugins like production software, not side projects.

Best Practices for Plugin Governance

- **Source Control:** Keep every plugin (Java, Groovy, or REST) in Git with version tags.
- **Testing:** Automate unit and regression tests in a staging environment mirroring production.
- **Review:** Enforce peer review before deployment — a second pair of eyes can save a weekend.
- **Change Freeze Policy:** Decide and document. Some clients freeze plugins 60 days pre-upgrade; others maintain CI/CD pipelines for continuous deployment. Choose based on your risk appetite, but be explicit.
- **Staging Discipline:** Always validate plugins against the next Collibra version before upgrade day. It's cheaper than an unplanned outage.

Reflective Note: Plugins are how Collibra becomes your Collibra – customized for your data culture and business processes. But innovation without guardrails quickly becomes chaos. Govern your extensions with the same rigor you apply to your data, and stability will follow naturally.

Workflow Engine Configuration: Turning Processes into Executable Code

When Collibra workflows first click into place, it feels almost magical. The policy that once lived in a PowerPoint slide now moves data between owners, sends notifications, and enforces accountability automatically. I still remember a global insurance client whose compliance officers used to chase approvals through endless email chains. Their first Collibra workflow – a simple policy certification process – cut the turnaround from ten days to two. From that moment, the platform stopped being "just a catalog" and started to feel like a living governance system.

Designing for Performance and Reliability

Behind that magic is a BPMN engine that behaves more like software than configuration. Treat it accordingly.

- Allocate thread pools with headroom for parallel task loads.
- Set retry policies for asynchronous steps to prevent silent failures.

- Validate transaction isolation levels so parallel approvals don't spawn duplicate tokens.
- Schedule periodic workflow audits to catch stalled instances before users notice.

Version Control and Release Discipline

Your workflows will evolve as business rules mature. Resist the urge to tweak them directly in production.

- Keep every BPMN file in source control (Git, Bitbucket).
- Use clear naming conventions tied to business domains (e.g., FIN_ApproveDefinition_v3).
- Deploy via pipeline: dev → test → stage → prod.
- Archive deprecated versions – nothing causes chaos faster than multiple workflows with similar names and overlapping logic.

Operational Hygiene

Workflows can clog if left unchecked.

- Monitor executor queues for buildup.
- Break long-running tasks into smaller, idempotent steps that can safely retry.
- Standardize log output and tag every workflow execution with a unique identifier for quick triage.

Reflective Note: A Collibra workflow is only as strong as the policy it automates. Don't model aspirational bureaucracy; model real human behavior. Every extra approval click you add today becomes another email tomorrow. The most elegant workflows I've seen were born from sitting beside stewards, watching how they actually do the job, and coding just enough automation to make it painless.

Data Lineage Configuration: Linking Technical Metadata with Business Context

Executives light up the first time they see a Collibra lineage diagram that actually mirrors reality. I remember a global bank where auditors used to spend weeks tracing a single metric from a regulatory report back to its data mart. When we switched on lineage and the arrows connected every transformation step from dashboard to source table, one manager leaned over and whispered, "That just saved us a month of audit prep." That's the power of getting lineage right – it turns skepticism into belief.

Harvesting Lineage Efficiently

Lineage works best when it's treated as part of your data plumbing, not an afterthought.

- Use Collibra Catalog or Edge for built-in harvesting; third-party tools can supplement for ETL or BI lineage.

- Deploy agents close to data sources to minimize latency and network overhead.
- Start with incremental harvesting schedules; reserve real-time ingestion for genuinely critical systems.
- Validate every new integration in a staging environment to ensure table names and IDs resolve correctly.

Stitching Business Meaning to Technical Reality

The hardest part isn't connecting systems – it's connecting semantics.

- Establish naming conventions that bridge physical and business terms (e.g., CUST_NBR → "Customer Identifier").
- Route ambiguous matches to curation workflows so humans review before relationships are published.
- Use glossary mappings and attribute-level documentation to explain "why this data exists," not just "where it moves."
- Regularly reconcile lineage diagrams with process documentation – drift happens quietly.

Managing Load and Index Health

Lineage ingestion can overwhelm your system if left unchecked.

- Throttle ingestion jobs to prevent queue backlogs and index lag.

- Separate "hot" tables refreshed hourly from "cold" tables updated nightly or weekly.
- Schedule reindexing during off-hours to keep search performance stable.
- Monitor index size and CPU trends; a sudden spike often signals runaway ingestion loops.

Reflective Note: A beautiful lineage graph isn't an end goal; it's a conversation starter. When users trace data flows themselves, they begin to trust – and question – data in productive ways. I once saw a finance analyst challenge a long-held KPI definition because lineage showed a hidden filter in the ETL logic. That debate led to a more accurate report and a culture that valued transparency over tradition. The real win of lineage isn't the diagram – it's the dialogue it sparks.

Backup, Recovery, and High Availability: Sleeping Well at Night

I've learned that nothing tests a governance team's discipline quite like an unexpected outage. The first time a Collibra environment I supported went down, it was a sleepy Saturday—until phones lit up because workflows had stalled mid-approval and auditors couldn't access certification logs. That weekend taught me what every platform lead eventually discovers: once Collibra becomes part of compliance and stewardship routines, it's no longer "just another app." It's a critical system of record, and your recovery plan determines whether you sleep soundly or not at all.

Backups that Actually Work

- Back up everything: the application repository, the search index, and uploaded attachments.
- Use native database tools such as pg_dump or Oracle RMAN for point-in-time recovery.
- Verify that backups capture configuration and custom plugins—not just metadata tables.
- Test restores quarterly in a separate environment. The test is the proof; backups without rehearsed restores are wishful thinking.

I once watched a company spend three days rebuilding an index because their backup script silently excluded the index directory. They now print the mantra above their operations desk: "Restore tests count more than backup jobs."

- **High Availability and Disaster Readiness**
- Deploy Collibra nodes in a cluster behind a load balancer to remove single points of failure.
- For on-prem setups, enable database replication and test failover between primary and standby instances.
- SaaS customers should confirm SLA coverage—understand exactly how Collibra handles redundancy.
- Document RTO (Recovery Time Objective) and RPO

(Recovery Point Objective) targets in a disaster-recovery runbook.

- Rehearse failovers. Some teams even gamify it—the "Wheel of Misfortune" drill, where engineers spin a wheel of disaster scenarios, is still the best training I've seen for keeping nerves steady when real alarms sound.

Reflective Note: Backups and clusters may sound like dry infrastructure topics, but they're the unsung foundation of data trust. Every minute of uptime tells your business users that governance is dependable. The ultimate compliment is silence—the platform hums, audits continue, and no one panics when a disk dies because your team already practiced the fix.

Monitoring and Observability: Seeing the Pulse of Governance

After one upgrade at a telecom client, the Collibra interface slowed to a crawl for half the users. Logs looked normal; servers looked fine. What cracked the case was a synthetic probe—a script that mimicked a user performing a catalog search every five minutes. It showed latency spiking exactly when nightly ETL jobs started. Once we tuned the indexing window, performance stabilized. That moment cemented my belief that observability isn't a luxury—it's your early-warning radar.

Collecting and Centralizing Metrics

- Expose Collibra's metrics via JMX, REST, or log streams; feed them into tools like Prometheus, Datadog, or Splunk.
- Track CPU, memory, thread counts, queue depths, error rates, and user response times.
- Add synthetic transactions—automated searches or workflow runs—to simulate user experience in real time.

Building Dashboards that Tell a Story

- Organize dashboards in three layers: Infrastructure, Application, and User Workflow.
- Correlate anomalies across layers—high CPU with steady workflow performance usually signals batch jobs, while rising latency with clean infrastructure metrics points to logic or plugin issues.
- Use color-coding and simple labels so non-technical stakeholders grasp system health instantly.

Alerting and Communication

- Align alert thresholds with business impact: two seconds of delay may be tolerable at midnight but critical during financial close.
- Adjust thresholds seasonally with feature flags or scripts.

- Share weekly health summaries with governance leadership; transparency builds confidence and justifies capacity investments.

Reflective Note: Monitoring isn't just about graphs—it's about credibility. When you can show that governance uptime, search latency, and workflow success rates are all trending positively, you signal maturity: A transparent dashboard becomes your quiet ambassador to the executive floor, proving that Collibra isn't merely installed—it's operated professionally.

Managing Environments: Dev, Test, Stage, and Prod

A Collibra implementation without disciplined environments is like flying an aircraft with no simulator. You don't want your first flight test to happen over a crowded city. I learned this the hard way years ago when a well-intentioned developer pushed an untested workflow change directly to production. Overnight, hundreds of certification tasks froze midstream. We spent two days unwinding it—and learned the golden rule: protect production at all costs.

Building the Four-Stage Pipeline

- Maintain separate Dev, Test, Stage, and Prod environments. Each exists for a purpose:
    - Dev - sandbox for experimentation and learning.
    - Test - validates configuration changes and workflows.

- Stage - replicates production as closely as possible; used for user acceptance and regression tests.
    - Prod - sacred ground for business operations only.
- Keep environments in lockstep. A change tested in Dev must pass through Test and Stage before touching Prod.

Promotion and Configuration as Code

- Use export/import scripts or the Collibra CLI/REST API to move configurations between environments.
- Treat metadata configuration like software—store versioned exports in source control (Git).
- Apply differential updates instead of full overwrites to minimize risk and downtime.
- Tag each promotion with a release version and change log for traceability.

Data Hygiene and Privacy

- When refreshing lower environments with production data, mask or redact sensitive fields—especially personally identifiable or financial information.
- If contractors or vendors access non-prod environments, verify masking before providing credentials.

Version Discipline

- Minimize version skew between environments; don't let Stage run one patch behind for long.
- Time-box deviations and document them. Even minor differences can produce misleading test results.
- When upgrading, apply patches first to Dev, then Test, Stage, and finally Prod, observing stability at each step.

Reflective Note: Managing environments may feel bureaucratic at first, but it's the heartbeat of operational reliability. Each tier gives your team a chance to make mistakes safely before real users ever notice. When you can promote a workflow from Dev to Prod with confidence–and no one in Finance even realizes a deployment happened—you've achieved quiet excellence.

Upgrade Strategy: Staying Current without Disruption

Upgrades are the governance equivalent of open-heart surgery–you want the new features, but you can't afford a skipped beat. I once worked with a financial firm that delayed Collibra upgrades for three years because "everything works fine." When the day finally came, half their custom plugins failed, the browser UI looked alien, and regression testing consumed six weeks. Their lesson–and mine–was clear: staying current is not vanity; it's survival.

Cadence and Rehearsal

- Plan two major upgrades per year, aligning one with Collibra's long-term support (LTS) cycle if possible.
- Rehearse the upgrade in Stage or a cloned environment—measure downtime, verify integrations, and time every step.
- Automate backups, schema migrations, and rollback scripts so you can reverse within minutes if something misfires.
- Record and publish the rehearsal results; they become your playbook for production.

Compatibility and Change Awareness

- Before every upgrade, review release notes and deprecation warnings. Pay attention to renamed endpoints, default setting changes, and any impact on plugins or API clients.
- Test integrations with external systems—especially authentication, workflow engine versions, and REST calls—to catch subtle mismatches early.
- Maintain a compatibility matrix that tracks Collibra versions, plugin versions, and dependent service versions side by side.

Communication and Enablement

- Announce upgrade windows well in advance. Share what's changing, why it matters, and when users can expect service interruptions.

- Provide a short "What's New" summary or two-minute screencast—users rarely read long emails, but they'll watch a quick demo.
- After the upgrade, open office hours or a live chat channel for early questions. It turns confusion into engagement.

Reflective Note: Upgrades test more than your technical readiness—they test organizational trust. When users see the platform evolve smoothly, confidence grows that governance is here to stay. The real victory is when an upgrade weekend passes quietly, the dashboards still glow green Monday morning, and your stewards notice only the small delights—a faster search bar, a cleaner form, a new icon that makes their day easier.

Governance of the Governance Platform: Change Control and Configuration Management

Collibra doesn't just enable governance—it needs governance itself. I learned that the hard way with a public-sector client whose administrators treated configuration changes like casual experiments. One afternoon, an eager analyst renamed an asset type directly in production to "make it clearer." Overnight, half the workflows failed because they couldn't find their expected asset type. The catalog recovered, but the damage to confidence took longer to heal. From then on, every Collibra change followed the same rigor as a code deployment.

Establish a Configuration Baseline

- Document every configurable element: communities, domains, asset types, workflows, roles, and custom attributes.
- Store that documentation (or export scripts) in a source-controlled repository such as Git.
- Tag each baseline with the Collibra version and deployment date. You can't manage drift if you don't know your starting point.

Define Change Control Processes

- Funnel all proposed changes through a lightweight Change Advisory Board (CAB)—often the same data governance council in a technical role.
- Require peer review for workflow or metamodel changes before implementation.
- Use lower environments—Dev, Test, Stage—as sandboxes. Promote through automated CI/CD pipelines or export/import scripts to minimize manual error.
- Maintain a change log visible to all administrators; transparency prevents accidental overwrites.

Version and Rollback Discipline

- Treat configuration like software. Apply semantic versioning to workflow and plugin releases (e.g., v2.3.1).
- Before each deployment, capture a snapshot of key XML and JSON configurations so you can revert fast.
- Regularly reconcile your running configuration against your Git baseline to detect drift.

Audit and Compliance Alignment

- Collibra's own audit logs are your ally. Include configuration changes in your periodic SOX or ISO audits.
- Set up alerts for high-impact operations–asset type edits, workflow deletions, or role modifications–to flag anomalies in real time.

Reflective Note: The irony of governance technology is that it can fall victim to the same chaos it was built to prevent. A disciplined change-control culture turns Collibra from a fragile prototype into an auditable, trustworthy enterprise platform. When your next audit asks, "Who approved this configuration change?" and you can answer within seconds–complete with timestamp and rollback plan—you'll know governance has truly come full circle.

Practitioner Stories: Voices from the Trenches

Every Collibra administrator carries battle scars–those late nights spent chasing invisible configuration bugs or fielding 2 a.m. calls when login screens refused to load. The stories that follow come from real projects where simple missteps taught lessons that still guide my approach today.

At a **large European bank**, performance deteriorated mysteriously two weeks after launch. Index rebuilds and extra CPUs did nothing. Only after a deep dive into query plans did we discover that a nightly ETL job was flooding the repository with redundant lineage records. Once the engineers refined the integration mappings, performance normalized. *The moral: optimize the workload before throwing hardware at the problem.*

A **North American retailer** faced a different kind of stall: the cybersecurity group mandated quarterly penetration tests. Collibra SaaS passed cleanly, but the scans flagged a third-party visualization plugin. Removing that plugin not only cleared the security audit but also halved average page-load times. *Lesson learned: security and performance often want the same things—leaner, simpler code paths.*

At a **global pharmaceutical company**, IT mapped Collibra roles directly to ITSM groups. When a steward resigned, their off-boarding ticket automatically revoked Collibra access. During the next audit cycle, the compliance team praised the seamless deprovisioning. *Automation, when done right, turns compliance from a chore into a quiet strength.*

Reflective note: These stories may seem ordinary in hindsight, but they represent the hidden victories that keep a governance platform healthy—the invisible fixes, the cautious optimizations, the simple automations that prevent chaos later.

Conclusion: Technical Bedrock for Governance Success

We have journeyed from choosing deployment topology to fine-tuning JVM flags, from auditing login attempts to rehearsing failover drills. By now it should be clear that a Collibra installation is not a matter of clicking Next on an installer. It is a disciplined craft—a blend of infrastructure engineering, security architecture, performance science, and change management.

Remember that technology serves people. The configurations we tuned today enable stewards to catalog data swiftly, analysts to discover definitions confidently, and executives to view lineage transparently. When the platform feels invisible yet indispensable, you have achieved technical maturity—the point where governance supports the business quietly and reliably.

Reflective Note: The best compliment you can receive as a Collibra administrator is silence—the absence of frantic emails, failed logins, and midnight restarts. It means the groundwork you laid is solid.

In the next chapter, we'll put that stability to work by onboarding real data assets and organizing them inside the catalog, where the results of all this invisible engineering finally become visible to the enterprise.

Chapter 8 Key Terms

Deployment Topology: The architectural setup of Collibra across environments (cloud, on-prem, hybrid).

SaaS (Software as a Service): A cloud-delivery model where software is hosted and managed by a provider.

Authentication: The process of verifying a user's identity, typically via SSO or SAML.

Authorization: Controlling what authenticated users can access or modify.

Version Control: Tracking and managing changes to configuration files and scripts.

Automation: Using scripts or tools to execute repetitive technical tasks automatically.

API Integration: Connecting systems through Application Programming Interfaces for metadata exchange.

Performance Tuning: Optimizing system parameters for speed and scalability.

Resilience: The ability of the system to recover quickly from failure or disruption.

9

Data Asset Onboarding And Cataloging

Bridging the Gap between Configuration and Content

When we wrapped up the technical configuration work in the last chapter, you and I left Collibra standing tall but mostly empty—like a brand-new library that still smells of fresh paint, waiting for its first shipment of books. The shelves are labelled, the catalog desk is polished, the librarians are trained, yet nothing truly valuable is inside until the books arrive and get properly cataloged. In Collibra, those books are your data assets. This chapter is about breathing life into the platform by onboarding and cataloging those assets in a way that makes them findable, trustworthy, and actionable from day one.

I still remember my first Collibra implementation back in 2015. We had installed the platform over a frenzied weekend, high-fived each other when the servers lit up, and then sat back on Monday morning facing an ocean of terabytes: data warehouses, lake buckets, BI reports, spreadsheets, and a mysterious folder called

"Do_Not_Delete_Archive." The question wasn't "how do we get it in?"—we knew the mechanics. The real question was "how do we get it in without losing control, so that people will actually use the catalog rather than bypass it?" This chapter distills the lessons learned from that and dozens of later rollouts to help you avoid the inevitable landmines.

Understanding What "Asset" Really Means

The word "asset" is one of those deceptively simple terms everyone nods at until they engage in their first onboarding workshop. That's when a report writer claims a dashboard is an asset, the data architect insists only tables count, and the data scientist waves a Jupyter notebook in the air like a white flag. In Collibra, an asset is anything you decide to govern. The platform is gloriously agnostic: if you can model it, you can govern it. What matters is drawing a line between what deserves to be in the enterprise catalog and what can remain in the dark corners of a shared drive.

Your line will be different from mine. A financial regulator may treat every single column in a transaction table as a governed asset because lineage and traceability are legally binding. A media company might only care about datasets that feed audience segmentation models because speed outweighs rigor. The critical takeaway is that you must decide consciously before you ingest. A good rule of thumb is to ask, "Would someone else in the organization search for this, rely on it for decision-making, or get in trouble if it's wrong?" If the answer is yes, it's an asset.

Automated Metadata Sources versus Human Knowledge

Once you know what qualifies, the next fork in the road is deciding how to capture metadata. Automation seduces with its promise of speed. Collibra's integration layer can harvest schemas and technical lineage from databases, ETL tools, BI platforms, and cloud services at the click of a button. Push that button and you can populate thousands of assets overnight. I've seen CIOs grin ear to ear watching dashboards fill with tables from Snowflake or S3.

Yet the euphoric moment often fizzles by morning. Automated harvesters bring in the raw ingredients–names, types, and relationships–but seldom capture context. A column labelled "CT" could be "Cycle Time" in manufacturing, "Counterparty Type" in trading, or simply "Connecticut" in customer addresses. The database has no idea. That's why human knowledge, often in the heads of stewards, analysts, and subject matter experts, remains irreplaceable. Collibra thrives on blending both: let the machines do the heavy lifting of discovery, then enlist humans to enrich, clarify, and certify.

Designing the Intake Pipeline

Think of onboarding as a pipeline with three major stages: discovery, enrichment, and publication. Discovery is where raw metadata surfaces, whether through automated harvest or manual entry. Enrichment is the value-add step—classifying data domains, adding business descriptions, tagging sensitivity, mapping lineage, and linking policies. Publication moves enriched assets into a consumer-friendly catalog zone, often after an approval or certification workflow.

Why bother with stages? Because experience shows that if you dump raw assets directly into the searchable catalog, you'll create chaos. Consumers will stumble over duplicates, cryptic names, and half-baked definitions, deciding Collibra is just another noisy tool. A gated pipeline keeps the messy middle away from everyday users while editors do their work. Picture a backstage door for performers before they dazzle the audience in the main hall.

Profiling and Enriching Metadata at Ingestion

One of the most eye-opening moments for new governance teams is running data profiling during onboarding. Collibra's Data Quality extensions or third-party scanners can compute simple statistics—null counts, min max, pattern frequencies—and surface anomalies. Suddenly, you see that "ZIP_CODE" accepts letters in 17 percent of rows, or that "DATE_OF_BIRTH" has a suspicious peak on January 1, 1900. Profiling isn't just a quality scorecard; it also feeds enrichment. If "ACCOUNT_BALANCE" never drops below zero, perhaps it's actually a "Credit Balance," and the name should reflect that nuance.

I like to sit with a data steward during the first profiling run and narrate what we're seeing, like a play-by-play commentator: "Do you notice how this numeric column has a standard deviation of zero? That means every row is identical. Maybe it's a flag field, not a measure." The aha moments that follow build both stewardship skills and confidence. In turn, that stewardship translates into richer, more reliable catalog entries.

Establishing Golden Sources and Avoiding Duplication

Nothing drains trust faster than duplicate assets. The problem is pernicious because modern data estates are rife with replicas—an operational copy in Postgres, a reporting copy in Redshift, and an ML-ready copy in Delta Lake, all carrying the same "CUSTOMERS" table. When you harvest from each platform, Collibra dutifully creates three assets. Which one should a business analyst use?

The solution is to declare a "golden" source of truth. Sometimes this is the original system of record; other times it's a curated layer in a warehouse. Collibra supports designation of authoritative assets through attributes or certifications. For example, you can set an asset status to Authoritative and configure search to rank authoritative results higher. Equally important, you can relate non-golden copies to their source through lineage, providing transparency without cluttering search results with near duplicates.

I once worked with a global pharma company where duplicate assays plagued the research pipeline. We added a simple "Reference Copy of" relationship in the model and made it mandatory for any derivative dataset. Within a month, researchers who had complained about "catalog noise" wrote to say they finally could trace data back to its lab of origin, saving weeks of verification.

The Steward's Desk: Best Practices for Manual Cataloging

While automation handles mass ingestion, some assets will always arrive by human hands. Think ad-hoc Excel models, one-off vendor files, or legacy PDFs that still matter. Here's how I coach stewards to handle them. First, never create an asset without a clear owner. An orphan asset is an abandoned puppy: everyone coos but no one feeds it. Second, write descriptions for a novice, not a veteran. If a new hire cannot grasp it within sixty seconds, refine. Third, link every manual asset to at least one governed data domain. Domains are Collibra's way of grouping assets by subject matter. Without them, your catalog becomes a junk drawer.

To ease the burden, encourage stewards to reuse glossary terms and policies. When they tag a dataset with a term that already exists, consumers gain instant cross-references, and search relevance improves. A steward who just "catalogs and forgets" may meet the letter of the process, but stewardship shines when they think like librarians connecting readers to broader knowledge.

A Practical Walkthrough: Onboarding a Snowflake Database

Let's roll up our sleeves and walk through a concrete scenario. Picture you manage the analytics environment for a retail chain. Your first candidate source is the Snowflake data warehouse that houses sales, inventory, and customer data. The goal is to make these assets discoverable for category managers planning holiday promotions.

We start by configuring the Snowflake driver in Collibra's Connectivity Console, entering the account URL, warehouse, and read-only credentials. Security teams typically give a narrow schema-level permission set, which avoids harvesting internal staging tables. Next, we schedule a harvest job, choosing the "Technical Data" option to pull schemas, tables, columns, and views. The initial run might discover five thousand tables and thirty thousand columns—enough to daunt any steward.

Collibra automatically assigns each asset a technical name like SNOWFLAKE.PUBLIC.SALES. At this stage, it's in the "Staging" domain, hidden from the wider user base. Our data domain leads now perform triage. They suppress ETL scratch tables, merge identical schemas used by test environments, and mark the primary "SALES" schema as authoritative. For columns, they rely on profiling to catch data types mismatches, then draft plain-English descriptions: "TOTAL_PRICE: Net selling price after discounts, in USD." They tag sensitive fields with "PII" or "PCI" terms from the glossary.

The final gate is a certification workflow. Two stewards and the business product owner must approve. When everyone signs off, the domain changes to "Approved Data Warehouse," making assets searchable to the retail planning team. I've seen the time from initial harvest to first business query shrink from months to two weeks with this pipeline. The secret isn't fancy tooling–it's a disciplined staging area and an engaged stewardship team.

Validation, Data Quality, and Certification

Certification deserves its own spotlight. Think of it as a quality seal on a jar of preserves: if done right, consumers will open and taste without fear. In Collibra, certification can be expressed through a status attribute, a workflow task, or a badge. Some organizations prefer a binary Certified Not Certified flag; others embrace multi-level statuses like Draft, Reviewed, Approved, Deprecated. The choice depends on how nuanced the governance process must be.

The power of certification lies in linking it to quantifiable data quality scores. Rather than a steward's gut feel, you can attach metrics such as completeness, validity, uniqueness, and timeliness pulled from data quality tools. I once embedded a rule that an asset could reach Certified only if null rate was below five percent for critical columns and lineage was fully documented back to source. Over time, assets that lacked the rigor languished in Draft, acting as gentle pressure on data owners to improve.

Capturing Lineage during Onboarding

Lineage has elevated from "nice to have" to "must have" in regulated industries and data-driven analytics shops alike. Capturing it during onboarding is far easier than retrofitting later. Automated scanners can extract lineage from ETL tools like Informatica, Matillion, or dbt and stitch together table-to-table links. However, business lineage—how a sales metric travels from transactional capture to executive dashboard—still requires human annotation.

Whenever possible, ask owners of ingestion pipelines to supply mapping docs or SQL transformations. Upload those as attachments to the data flow diagram in Collibra. Even if automation covers eighty percent, that twenty percent of manual commentary often contains the breakthroughs analysts search for: "We exclude gift card redemptions from net sales," or "We convert all prices to USD at daily xe.com rates." Those nuggets matter to forecasting teams and auditors alike.

Handling Sensitive Data Classification and Privacy

The first time GDPR fines loomed over a client, the request came in hot: "Show me everywhere customer birth date is stored within forty-eight hours." Without a catalog, the task would take weeks. With Collibra, the speed of answer depends on whether data classification was embedded in onboarding. If you mark sensitive columns with personally identifiable information tags the day they enter Collibra, the privacy office can run a simple domain search and generate a heat map in minutes.

Tagging sensitive data can be automated via pattern matching—detecting columns named *_SSN or containing nine-digit numeric patterns—but don't rely on it exclusively. Finance systems may label Social Security Number as "NATIONAL_ID" or even cryptic codes. A steward's domain knowledge fills gaps. The best practice is dual verification: automated tagging plus human review. When privacy teams trust the tagging rigor, they advocate for Collibra adoption rather than policing it from the sidelines.

Governing the Long Tail: Spreadsheets, Reports, and Shadow IT

Every enterprise fights the same three-headed monster: spreadsheets, rogue reports, and shadow databases nobody admits exist. They live outside sanctioned platforms yet drive critical decisions. How do you onboard such unruly assets without drowning in manual work?

The trick is to prioritize business impact over exhaustive coverage. Identify "high-value" spreadsheets—those sent to executives, used in regulatory filings, or referenced during quarterly earnings. Collibra's file import wizard can scan folder hierarchies and create an asset per file, capturing basic metadata automatically. Then, schedule focused workshops where analysts annotate the handful of worksheets and pivot tables that matter the most. You might catalog only twenty percent of artifacts but cover eighty percent of decision-making surface area.

Shadow IT databases pose a different challenge—often they exist precisely because legitimate data channels are slow. Treat onboarding as a carrot, not a stick. Offer project teams a path to recognition: if they let you catalog their database, they gain visibility and support without surrendering autonomy. Over time, the catalog acts like gravity, pulling satellite systems toward the orbit of governed data rather than pushing them away.

Change Detection and Incremental Harvesting

Data warehouses evolve. Columns get added, tables renamed, schemas split. The first harvest is the easy part; staying in sync is harder. Collibra's incremental harvesting can detect changes since the last run and update only affected assets. But automation can't decide whether a change is benign or business-critical. A new column capturing marketing consent might be essential for privacy compliance, whereas splitting a lookup table may be irrelevant to most users.

That's why change detection should feed into a stewardship notification workflow. When a schema change triggers, stewards receive a digest summarizing additions, deletions, and modifications. They triage, enrich, and re-publish. The cadence depends on velocity of change. High-churn data lakes might harvest nightly, whereas stable finance warehouses harvest weekly. Align frequency with the threshold at which stale metadata poses risk.

Keeping the Catalog Fresh: Recertification Cycles

Left unchecked, certifications expire in spirit long before they expire in status. I once found a "Certified" dataset whose source system had been decommissioned six months earlier. The badge remained, mocking the very idea of governance. To prevent such decay, incorporate automatic recertification cycles. For example, set certifications to expire every ninety days unless a steward re-affirms.

Collibra supports timed workflows that reopen approval tasks or move assets to a "Needs Review" status. This nudge ensures owners look at data with fresh eyes, update descriptions, adjust quality scores, and confirm lineage accuracy. Consumers, in turn, trust that a green checkmark means something current, not institutional inertia.

Case Study: A Global Retailer's Journey

A global retailer I worked with faced classic catalog chaos. They operated in thirty countries, each with its own Oracle database, plus a consolidated Snowflake warehouse. Analysts wasted days reconciling numbers between local and global reports. We launched an onboarding program starting with the five countries generating seventy percent of revenue.

Automated Oracle harvests produced forty-eight thousand table assets. We initially gasped—the steward team was only four people. Instead of brute-forcing enrichment, we set criteria: an asset would be curated only if referenced by an ETL job feeding Snowflake or by a Tableau workbook cited in monthly ops meetings. That trimmed the scope to three thousand tables. We staged them, launched profiles, and held daily two-hour "metadata sprints," where stewards sat with domain experts. After two weeks, core sales and inventory data were certified. As soon as executives saw unified definitions in the catalog, they pressured the remaining countries to join. What began as an impossible mountain turned into a virtuous cycle of demand pulling supply.

Metrics That Matter during Asset Onboarding

You can't improve what you don't measure. During onboarding, the key metrics I track are coverage, enrichment depth, and time to certification. Coverage is the percentage of critical systems represented in Collibra. Enrichment depth looks at attributes filled versus mandatory; if every table has a business description and owner, you're golden. Time to certification measures how quickly new or changed assets move from discovery to publish. When the metric slips, it's usually a sign that stewards are overloaded or the workflow is too onerous.

Once, our time-to-certification ballooned from seven to twenty days. We discovered that stewards spent half their time chasing owners for approvals. We streamlined the workflow: assets auto-certified if owners failed to act within five business days, subject to weekly audit. Paradoxically, accountability improved because nobody wanted their inaction recorded.

Lessons Learned and Quick Wins

If there's one lesson to engrave on your coffee mug, it's this: onboarding is not a one-off project stage but a perpetual heartbeat. Treat it as an always-on process, and Collibra will stay alive rather than fossilize. Start with assets that answer a burning business question, ensure they are enriched and certified, and let success market itself. Resist the urge to boil the ocean. It's better to govern one lake you actually swim in than to draw a map of every puddle no one touches.

Another quick win: surface the catalog where users already work. Embedding Collibra search in Tableau or Power BI means a user seeking a report clicks a side panel rather than logging into another app. Adoption rises, and the value of onboarding becomes self-evident.

Transitioning to Workflows and Automation

We have filled our library with books, each meticulously cataloged and stamped with quality seals. But librarians don't just shelve books—they facilitate circulation, track due dates, and acquire new titles. In the Collibra world, those tasks translate into workflows and automation, which orchestrate how data moves, transforms, and gets approved across the enterprise. Now that you and I have mastered onboarding, it's time to step behind the curtain and design the processes that will keep this catalog humming without constant human babysitting. That journey begins in the next chapter.

Chapter 9 Key Terms

Data Asset Onboarding: The process of adding new datasets or systems into the governance catalog.

Cataloging: Systematically organizing and documenting data assets with metadata.

Data Lineage: End-to-end trace of data flow from origin to consumption.

Quality Rule: A standard used to measure and monitor data integrity.

Certification: A formal approval that a dataset meets quality and governance standards.

Stewardship Review: Periodic validation of metadata accuracy and completeness.

Golden Source: The authoritative dataset recognized as the single source of truth.

Curation: The continuous refinement and enrichment of catalog content

10

Building Workflows And Automation

I will never forget the first time I watched a freshly cataloged data asset glide through an approval workflow in Collibra. Only a week earlier, the same asset had languished in a shared spreadsheet, waiting for someone—anyone—to acknowledge its existence. At that moment, though, the Catalog page lit up with a green checkmark, an audit log captured every decision, and a notification pinged the business owner. Something had shifted: our data governance program had moved from static documentation to living process. In the last chapter you and I explored the mechanics of onboarding data sets, business terms, and technical metadata. Now the question becomes: how do we turn that raw inventory into a self-regulating system that reinforces policy, accelerates collaboration, and scales effortlessly? The answer sits at the heart of Collibra's workflow and automation framework.

The Promise of a Self-Driving Governance Program

Picture yourself back in the days when most governance processes unfolded in email threads. A data steward opened a ticket. A domain lead asked for context. The security team weighed in on classification. By the time the conversation wrapped up, half the people had missed a crucial reply buried three messages deep. Decisions were undocumented or trapped in an archive folder. The result: frustrated users, unclear lineage, and constant rework. Collibra's designers recognized that governance has to be more than a repository; it must embed itself in day-to-day operations, guiding users, capturing institutional knowledge, and enforcing policy without forcing heroic manual effort. Workflows transform what would otherwise be documentation into an active governance fabric.

Because you invested time in Chapter 9 to import, profile, and relate your assets, you now hold the foundational metadata objects. Those objects are the actors in the story, but they need scripts, stages, and cues. Think of workflows as the choreography that dictates how data moves, who intervenes, and which controls illuminate compliance checkpoints. Automation, in turn, is the moment the curtain rises and the show runs by itself under the watchful eye of a small backstage crew. Your goal during this chapter is to learn not just how to draw arrows in a BPMN diagram but how to embed the values of your governance operating model–stewardship, accountability, transparency–directly into executable code.

A Quick Walk Through Collibra's Workflow Engine

Before we dive into the creative craft, let's demystify the technology. Collibra employs an embedded Apache-based process engine that interprets standards-compliant BPMN 2.0 models. When you open the Workflow Designer, you will see familiar shapes: start events, user tasks, service tasks, gateways, timers, and end events. Drag them onto the canvas, connect them with sequence flows, and the engine will translate that visual logic into an executable process definition. Behind the scenes, a Java-based runtime persists the state of every workflow instance, exposes variables through RESTful endpoints, and logs history tables for auditability. All of that is transparent to the business user, who experiences only a friendly form, a to-do inbox, or an email reminder.

Yet technology alone does not guarantee a successful automation program. The real art is mapping each step to an organizational need. If you have spent time with agile story mapping, you already know the power of narrative. A user wants to achieve an outcome, so the system provides a path. In Collibra the story might read: "As a data steward, I want to certify a data set, so consumers can trust its quality." The moment you write that sentence, you can translate it into a workflow: intake, validation, peer review, certification, publication. At each boundary, you decide whether to ask for human judgment or to call an automatic rule. Let me share a personal example from a healthcare client. They struggled with physician names stored inconsistently across hospital systems. A stewardship team created a "Provider Record Certification" workflow that automatically matched names against an authoritative registry. If the algorithm found no match or multiple matches, the workflow escalated to a data custodian. The custodian's decision looped back to update the certification status. Physicians soon found their schedule-management app populating accurate provider IDs, without ever learning the name of the workflow that made it happen.

Translating Governance Policies into BPMN Diagrams

When you sit down to design, start with policy rather than technology. Governance policies articulate who is accountable, what standards must be met, when assessments occur, and how exceptions are handled. Each policy can become a top-level process with subprocesses that mirror control objectives. Suppose your policy says that any critical data element must undergo quarterly attestation. You could schedule a timer event that launches an "Attestation Request" workflow every ninety days. The start event then creates user tasks for each domain steward, prepopulated with the list of critical elements. The steward reviews the attributes, confirms or updates lineage links, and signs off. A gateway checks whether any elements were changed. If yes, the workflow triggers a recalculation of quality scores and notifies downstream system owners. If no changes, the workflow ends but stores an audit entry showing that the review occurred. By embedding the timer, user task, and gateway logic, you have essentially encoded the policy into software.

Let's take another example that is close to my heart: privacy impact assessments. A global media company I worked with had to comply with both GDPR and CCPA. Their privacy office wrote a policy dictating that any new data processing activity must undergo a DPIA before moving to production. We modeled the policy in three layers. Layer one was a "New Processing Activity Intake" form, launched by a developer or product manager. Layer two routed the submission through decision gateways based on the type of personal data and the geographic scope. If the activity involved special categories under GDPR, the workflow automatically forked to create a subtask for the Data Protection Officer. If the scope included ad-tech cookies, it forked to the legal counsel. Layer three handled outcomes: approve, revise, or reject. Because the entire process was captured in Collibra, auditors could trace each processing activity from inception to sign-off without opening a single email archive.

Choosing the Right Moments to Automate

Every organization is tempted to automate everything. Resist that urge. Automation pays dividends only when the underlying process is stable and when system-driven actions outperform human judgment on speed, accuracy, or compliance. During early maturity stages, you might keep certain decisions manual so that you can observe real-world usage and adjust criteria. A common mistake I see is to automate data quality rule deployments before stewards understand which rules matter most. The result is a barrage of alerts that desensitizes users. Start with a human-centric workflow that surfaces issues, let stewards classify severity, and then gradually introduce automatic severity scoring.

Think of automation in concentric circles. At the core are repetitive, deterministic tasks: field mapping, lineage stitching, license expiration reminders. Those are low-risk opportunities ripe for service tasks. In the next circle lie semi-structured decisions, such as approving glossary term definitions. You can partly automate them by pre-filling forms with suggestions and letting a human click approve. The outer circle holds complex, context-rich decisions like sanctioning a new AI model. In those cases, automation's role is to orchestrate collaboration, not to substitute for expert judgment. Model the process, capture the artifacts, but leave the conclusion to a committee.

Designing User-Centric Workflows

When I first began sketching processes, I focused on the system's vantage point: which fields to update, which statuses to set. Users complained that the forms felt like bureaucratic hoops. I realized that a successful workflow should feel invisible, surfacing only the minimum information at each step. In Collibra the Form Builder lets you control field visibility by role or condition. For a fortune-500 retailer, we built a "Product Attribute Onboarding" workflow. Analysts only saw the business description and usage fields. Technical data engineers saw source system, schema, and load frequency. Compliance officers saw classification flags. The same instance presented a personalized interface to each participant, reducing cognitive overload.

The second pillar of user-centric design is timing. If tasks arrive at awkward moments, users perceive them as interruptions. One trick I learned from agile ceremonies is to align governance tasks with existing cadences. Most teams have weekly sprints or recurring business reviews. Schedule your workflow timers to create tasks on Monday morning, never Friday afternoon. Collibra supports due dates and reminders. A well-timed reminder often matters more than any fancy screen.

A third pillar is language. Replace jargon like "asset" or "resource" with domain-specific terms that resonate with users. In financial services, call it "instrument." In marketing, call it "campaign list." Forms offer translation keys; you can label fields according to context while keeping the underlying attribute names. That small touch converts resistance into adoption, because users feel the system speaks their dialect.

Prototyping, Testing, and Iterating

You do not need to build a perfect workflow on day one. Collibra's Workflow Designer supports versioning. Start with a minimum viable process: a start event, one user task, and an end event. Deploy it, invite a few friendly stewards to test, and watch the audit logs. Collibra's built-in process monitor lets you inspect tokens, variables, and durations. If you notice tasks stalling, explore why. Maybe a role assignment is too narrow or a form forgot to map a variable. Iterate quickly. The beauty of versioning is that existing instances keep running on their deployed definition while new instances pick up the improved logic. You never disrupt ongoing work.

During one government project, we discovered that a lineage enrichment service failed silently when a field contained null values. Because we had wrapped that service in a try-catch block inside the workflow, the user never saw an error; they just wondered why lineage was blank. We inserted a logging gateway that captured service responses and exposed them in an admin dashboard. Suddenly we could spot patterns: certain legacy systems sent malformed XML. We fed that insight back to the ingestion team, all thanks to instrumentation baked into the workflow. Testing is not merely a quality gate; it is a feedback loop that sharpens your governance program.

Case Study: Data Quality Issue Resolution Workflow

Let me walk you through a full example that illustrates the power of orchestrated automation. A multinational manufacturer struggled with inconsistent units of measure across ERP systems. Kilograms, pounds, and tons appeared interchangeably, breaking business intelligence reports. The governance charter mandated a data quality process, but execution was manual, reliant on Slack messages. We designed a "Data Quality Issue Resolution" workflow.

The start event was a service task listening to an external data quality monitoring tool via API. Whenever the tool's rule flagged an anomaly, it called Collibra with a payload containing asset ID, rule ID, threshold, and sample records. The service task created a new Issue object in Collibra and launched a token.

A gateway checked whether the rule already had an open issue. If yes, the workflow attached evidence to the existing issue and exited. If no, it created a user task for the domain steward. The form pre-populated severity using historical resolution times and business impact scores. Because the manufacturer had invested in a maturity model, we could compute severity automatically based on policy thresholds; the steward could override, but rarely did.

Once the steward acknowledged the issue, the workflow branched. For low severity, it waited three working days for resolution. For medium or high severity, it escalated immediately to a data owner. All timing was handled by intermediate timer events. Resolution required the steward to provide a root-cause category chosen from a controlled vocabulary: source system, mapping, transformation, data entry, external feed. That entry powered the governance council's quarterly trend analysis.

When the steward clicked resolve, the workflow ran a service task that re-executed the original data quality rule via API. If the tool returned zero anomalies, the workflow closed and recorded success metrics in a custom dashboard. If anomalies persisted, the gateway looped back, creating another task and logging the failed attempt. The loop enforced accountability without punishing the steward; the log clearly distinguished between fix attempts and systemic failures. Over six months, average resolution time dropped from ten days to two, and the organization saved hundreds of analyst hours.

Extending Capabilities with Decision Tables and Service Tasks

BPMN gateways provide powerful branching, but sometimes you need more nuanced logic. Collibra supports decision tables through DMN or through embedded scripting. A decision table resembles a spreadsheet where each row defines conditions and outcomes. For example, in a "Data Sharing Request" workflow, you might have a decision table that checks data classification, requester role, and purpose of use. The outcome might assign the approval task to legal, security, or business owner, or combine them for joint approval. By externalizing the decision logic, you let non-technical policy owners update rules without redeploying the workflow. In practice, your legal counsel can open the decision table, add a row stating that any request involving biometrics must route to privacy officers, save, and new instances will adhere to that policy instantly.

Service tasks are the beating heart of automation. They call external APIs, execute scripts, or interact with Collibra's own REST endpoints. One media client uses a service task to generate anonymized sample data via a synthetic data generator. When a data scientist requests access to a sensitive data set, the workflow launches the generator, attaches the sample file to the request, and the scientist can explore structure without waiting for production access approval. That small piece of automation cut lead time from weeks to minutes.

Another example is licensing compliance. A financial firm had purchased Demographic Data bundles from an external vendor. License terms required quarterly reporting of user counts. We built a schedule that ran a service task every quarter. The task queried Collibra for user roles, counted how many users had access to the data set, generated a CSV, and emailed it to the vendor's portal. Zero manual intervention. Compliance at the press of a button—or rather, no button at all.

Integrating Workflows with External Systems

Chapter 11 will dive deeply into integration patterns, but you can already start thinking about how workflows act as orchestration layers across your data ecosystem. Collibra provides out-of-the-box connectors and a robust REST API, yet the pattern remains the same: a service task issues an HTTP request, processes the response, and updates workflow variables. The beauty is that you can fungibly swap endpoints: JDBC metadata ingestion, Snowflake governance tags, Tableau workbook ownership, ServiceNow ticket creation.

In a cloud migration project, we needed to synchronize data classifications between Collibra and AWS Glue. We modeled a "Classification Sync" workflow. A daily timer fired, the workflow queried Collibra assets tagged as "Synced," collected their classifications, and passed the payload to a Lambda function. The Lambda function updated corresponding Glue catalog tables. If the API returned errors, the workflow spawned a user task for the data platform engineer with the JSON error log attached. The integration eliminated outages caused by mismatched classifications, and the audit trail lived entirely within Collibra.

Because the workflow engine can call out, it can also receive calls. You can start workflows via API from external triggers: a Spark job finishing, a CI CD pipeline deploying a new schema, or a chatbot receiving a data request. This bidirectional communication demonstrates that Collibra is not merely a console but a governance control plane woven into operational fabric.

Governing the Governance: Controls Within Workflows

It is easy to create a tangle of processes that no one understands. Governance applies to workflows themselves. Establish versioning policies: who can deploy, who can deactivate, who can modify forms. Collibra roles such as Workflow Designer, Global Admin, and Domain Admin delineate authority. I recommend naming conventions that embed version numbers and release dates in process IDs. For example, DQ_Issue_Resolution_v2_2023-09-15. That naming pattern, coupled with release notes stored in a Collibra community, helps auditors trace which logic applied to which instance.

Another control is separation of duties. Developers should not be the same users who approve their own deployments. Use Collibra's staging environments: design in dev, test in QA, promote to prod. Each promotion is itself a governance event that you can model as a workflow, capturing reviews, sign-offs, and rollback plans.

Finally, monitor performance metrics. Collibra exposes workflow engine statistics: average task completion time, number of active instances, error counts. Build dashboards that map these metrics back to KPIs defined in Chapter 13. For example, if average approval cycle time exceeds policy targets, investigate whether workload is unbalanced or form length is excessive.

Measuring Workflow Performance

You cannot improve what you do not measure. The simplest metric is throughput: how many instances completed, how many aborted. More insightful is lead time: start to finish. Cycle time per task pinpoints bottlenecks. For machine-triggered processes, measure success rate of service calls. For human tasks, measure bounce rate: how often a task is reassigned because roles are misconfigured.

Return to the data quality example. We tracked mean time to resolution weekly. Within six weeks, we had baseline figures. We noticed that escalation tasks sat untouched on weekends. Policy stipulated twenty-four-hour SLA, but weekend lapses violated that. We adjusted timers to exclude weekends, then published the SLA in the user task header so stewards saw a countdown. Compliance improved by thirty percent. Without data, we would have blamed people; with data, we optimized process.

Visualization matters. Collibra Insights or BI tools fed by the Collibra Data Dictionary allow you to plot lead time histograms, cumulative flow diagrams, and SLA trend lines. Storytelling through dashboards converts abstract numbers into compelling evidence for investment: more training, additional headcount, or re-engineered forms.

Common Mistakes and How to Avoid Them

I have stubbed my toe on every possible rock in this path. The first mistake is over-modeling. New designers cram every exception path into one monster diagram. Users stare at forms thirty fields long and give up. Instead, apply Occam's Razor: build the simplest workflow that satisfies ninety percent of cases; handle rare exceptions manually until they justify their own subprocess.

The second mistake is forgetting security. Service tasks often require credentials to call external systems. Store those credentials in secure properties, not hard-coded scripts. Rotate them; audit them.

Third, ignore change management at your peril. If you deploy a new workflow overnight, you may break existing integrations or frustrate stewards who were mid-task. Communicate release dates, provide sandbox environments, and document changes.

Fourth, neglect performance. A process that loops over thousands of assets may exhaust database connections. Batch operations or use asynchronous tasks.

Finally, let me confess a personal blunder. At a telecom company, I wired a gateway to auto-close data quality issues if they stayed unresolved for thirty days, thinking it would reset stale tickets. Instead, executives interpreted closed tickets as fixed issues. I had inadvertently masked problems instead of exposing them. We removed the auto-close and replaced it with periodic reminders plus escalation to a director. Transparency triumphed over tidiness.

Continuous Improvement Through Feedback Loops

Workflows are living organisms. As business evolves—new regulations, mergers, system upgrades—your processes must adapt. Establish a quarterly review cycle where stewards, owners, compliance officers, and developers analyze metrics and user feedback. Each iteration may spawn user stories feeding into the agile backlog you learned to manage in Chapter 5. Deploy updated versions, retire obsolete ones, and archive instances per retention policy.

One insurance client gamified stewardship duties. They tracked how many tasks each steward completed and displayed leaderboards. Productivity soared but also surfaced concerns about quality. We added peer review steps proportional to task count. The lesson: metrics drive behavior; use them thoughtfully.

Conclusion: From Workflow to Ecosystem

You and I began this chapter acknowledging that cataloged assets alone do not guarantee governed data. We explored how Collibra's workflow engine converts static metadata into dynamic, policy-driven processes. We discussed mapping policies to BPMN diagrams, designing user-centric forms, selecting appropriate automation boundaries, integrating with external systems, and governing the workflows themselves. By embedding decision logic, timers, and service tasks, you can craft a self-driving governance program that scales beyond human bandwidth while honoring human oversight.

As you deploy these workflows, you will inevitably encounter integration touchpoints—APIs to data quality tools, BI dashboards, ticketing systems, cloud catalogs. In the next chapter, we will take a deeper dive into those integration strategies, examining how Collibra interfaces with the broader data ecosystem to maintain synchronized metadata and reinforce the automation you have just built. Your workflows are the choreography; integrations are the orchestra. Let's tune those instruments together in Chapter 11.

Chapter 10 Key Terms

Workflow Automation: Designing and executing automated governance processes.

BPMN (Business Process Model and Notation): An international standard for describing process workflows.

Approval Process: A structured sequence ensuring that data changes receive necessary sign-offs.

Certification Workflow: A process that validates and approves data assets for official use.

Exception Handling: Mechanisms to manage workflow errors or policy violations.

Notification Engine: The Collibra component that alerts users about tasks and events.

Process Efficiency: A metric evaluating time and effort saved through automation.

11

Integrating Collibra With Your Data Ecosystem

A Bridge from Workflows to the Wider World

In the last chapter we took a deep dive into workflows and automation, discovering how Collibra's process engine can shepherd data issues from discovery to resolution without human bottlenecks. By now you can picture a bustling governance hub where stewards raise flags, custodians approve changes, and quality rules fire off like clockwork. Yet, if that hub remains sealed off from the technology landscape surrounding it, the cadence will falter. A workflow is only as reliable as the data it orchestrates, and that data lives across warehouses, lakes, BI dashboards, machine-learning notebooks, and operational applications.

So, the natural next step is to open the doors. In this chapter I want to walk you through the art and discipline of integrating Collibra with the broader ecosystem that fuels your organization's insights. We will explore architectural choices, technical options, design patterns, and the subtle human considerations that turn point-to-point scripts into sustainable value chains. I will share the scars and triumphs from projects where I have sat in war rooms, negotiated with security teams, and celebrated the moment a lineage diagram lit up for the first time. By the time we wrap up, you should feel comfortable charting an integration roadmap and defending it when tough questions arise during steering-committee meetings.

Why Integration Determines Governance Success

I often open integration workshops with a simple question: "If Collibra vanished tomorrow, would anyone outside the governance team notice?" When silence follows, the problem is obvious. Collibra must embed itself so deeply into daily data activities that its absence would cripple analytics, regulatory reporting, or customer personalization. Integration is the mechanism by which that embedment occurs.

First, automated ingestion keeps the catalog fresh. No steward can manually register thousands of new tables created by an overnight ingestion job in a cloud warehouse. When metadata flows in continuously, stakeholders trust that what they see in Collibra mirrors reality.

Second, bi-directional synchronization turns the catalog into more than a read-only encyclopedia. Imagine a data scientist requesting access to a restricted dataset. If Collibra pushes the approved request straight into the access management system, the scientist experiences governance as a helpful concierge, not a gatekeeper. Conversely, when a column is masked in the warehouse due to new privacy guidance, that change must ripple back into Collibra so policies, classifications, and lineage remain accurate.

Finally, integration is crucial for advanced capabilities such as impact analysis. A risk officer cannot evaluate the blast radius of a broken metric unless lineage diagrams reach seamlessly from report objects in Tableau, through semantic layers, into SQL transformations, and down to raw source feeds. That continuity only exists when every link along the chain is integrated.

Mapping Your Data Landscape before Writing a Line of Code

Before touching an API, take stock of the terrain. In my first large-scale Collibra rollout, I skipped this step. Weeks later the backlog was littered with ad-hoc connector requests, each pulling in conflicting metadata structures. We had to halt the project and draw a proper map.

Start with the major system categories. There are source systems under operational control, integration layers where data is staged or transformed, analytic platforms where insights are consumed, and governance or security tools enforcing rules along the way. Within each category, note both the technology stacks and the business processes that depend on them. It is not enough to know that Snowflake is your warehouse; you must also understand that Finance closes the books on the third business day and loads sensitive GL data at five a.m. That timing affects when metadata extraction can occur without locking tables.

Next, identify ownership and connectivity constraints. Some systems fall under central IT, some under business units, and others under third-party providers. Each ownership model dictates a different approval path for API credentials, network access, and maintenance windows. I have seen projects stall because a SaaS vendor needed six weeks to provision a service account. Plot these constraints early so your critical path remains realistic.

Finally, classify systems by integration priority. Criteria include regulatory impact, project dependencies, data volume, and strategic importance. During one engagement, we focused first on a modest-sized customer relationship management platform because a looming GDPR audit required transparent consent tracking. That quick win bought political capital to tackle the sprawling data lake later.

Choosing the Right Integration Strategy

Collibra offers several mechanisms, and selecting the correct blend requires balancing immediate requirements with long-term sustainability. The main options are the REST API, Collibra Import and Export, the lineage harvester, and Collibra Connect powered by

MuleSoft. You can also write custom scripts or leverage partner connectors.

The REST API is the Swiss Army knife. It exposes every entity, attribute, relation, and workflow state. I often use it for targeted automation, such as updating ownership when a team restructures. The challenge is that the API is low level. You manage pagination, concurrency, and error handling yourself. If you are ingesting millions of objects, you will need robust back-off logic to avoid throttling.

Collibra Import and Export, based on CSV or Excel templates, shines for initial bulk loads or for ad-hoc updates where API coding overhead is unwarranted. You define communities, domains, and assets in rows and upload them through the UI. The rigidity of column naming can trip up newcomers, but once you master the pattern, it is surprisingly powerful. One hospital client keeps a parametric template that business analysts fill weekly to onboard new HL7 feeds without waiting for IT.

The lineage harvester tackles technical lineage, scanning code repositories, ETL jobs, and SQL scripts to extract transformation logic. It is indispensable when you must produce end-to-end flows for auditors. Yet, the harvester alone does not classify data or set policies. It works best in concert with other ingestion methods.

Collibra Connect is the enterprise integration platform. Built on MuleSoft, it offers pre-built connectors to popular systems such as

Snowflake, SAP, Informatica, and Tableau. The drag-and-drop interface lowers the barrier for teams unfamiliar with Java or Python. More importantly, its orchestration capabilities allow you to chain together complex pipelines, route errors, and enforce SLAs. On a global retail project we orchestrated nightly ingest jobs across five regions, each respecting local data residency rules, through a single Connect runtime.

Custom scripts remain a viable option when unique file formats or near-real-time requirements exist. I once wrote a Python daemon that listened to Apache Kafka topics and pushed new schema changes to Collibra within seconds. That speed was essential for a fraud detection platform where stale metadata could lead to false negatives.

A hybrid approach usually wins. You might rely on Connect for standard assets, supplement with API calls for niche systems, and run the harvester monthly to refresh lineage. The key is documenting which tool handles which domain so that future maintainers are not guessing.

Designing for Scale and Performance

Integration harms no one at pilot scale; problems surface when the nightly job balloons from twenty to two hundred systems. Performance tuning starts with understanding Collibra's internal model. Every asset, attribute, and relation is stored in a graph database. Graphs handle complex relationships elegantly, but they can be sensitive to write patterns. If your ingestion blasts millions of nodes in a single transaction, you will lock resources and impact users.

Chunking workloads is your friend. In one implementation we processed tables alphabetically, committing every thousand assets. Between commits we paused long enough for garbage collection to finish, then resumed. The total run time remained acceptable, and the platform stayed responsive.

Indexing also matters. Collibra uses Lucene under the hood for search. When ingesting large volumes, schedule re-indexing during quiet hours or use incremental indexing flags. I once let a lineage import trigger a full index rebuild at midday; the entire organization lost search capability for half an hour.

Network throughput can surprise you. Collibra Connect running on-premises against a cloud Collibra instance will bottleneck if outbound bandwidth is limited. Measure sustained transfer rates during testing and, if needed, deploy Connect runtimes closer to the target platform.

Finally, purge stale metadata periodically. A telco client saw performance degrade because nightly ingestion jobs appended new table versions without retiring decommissioned ones. We introduced a retention policy that archived assets after six months of inactivity. Search speed doubled, and user satisfaction soared.

Crafting a Robust Security Model

Security teams are rightfully cautious when you propose a new integration that reads from sensitive systems or writes back policy decisions. The secret to a smooth security review lies in preparation.

First, articulate data flows clearly. On one banking project we produced swim-lane diagrams showing that Collibra only pulled schema definitions, never row-level data. That single slide quelled concerns about insider trading violations.

Second, adopt the principle of least privilege. Create service accounts that can fetch metadata but cannot alter production tables. When writing back to operational systems, scope permissions narrowly. For example, a workflow might update a mask flag in a masking rules table and nothing else.

Third, secure credentials. Collibra Connect allows externalization of secrets into a vault so they never appear in source control. If you build custom code, rely on cloud secret managers or hardware security modules. Do not store passwords in plaintext properties files; auditors will find them. I learned this the hard way during a SOC 2 audit when we had to revamp a dozen scripts over a weekend.

Fourth, consider tokenization or data minimization when transporting metadata. If a field's business name contains personally identifiable information, redacting or hashing it before transfer can simplify compliance.

Finally, log everything. Both Collibra and integration platforms emit audit trails. Retain them in a centralized logging solution so incidents can be reconstructed swiftly. During an investigation at a pharmaceutical company, we traced an unauthorized schema export back to a misconfigured integration job within minutes because detailed logs were available.

Error Handling and Resilience

Even the most elegant integration pipeline will encounter timeouts, schema drift, or credential expirations. Resilience is the hallmark of a mature implementation.

Start with idempotency. If a job fails halfway, rerunning it should not create duplicates or orphaned relations. Use natural keys like system name and technical name rather than surrogate identifiers when constructing asset codes. Collibra will match existing assets and update them instead of inserting new ones.

Implement retries with exponential back-off. Collibra's API returns HTTP status codes that guide recovery. A 429 indicates rate limiting; pausing and trying again later usually suffices. By contrast, a 4xx authentication error demands immediate human intervention, so route it to an alerting queue.

Differentiate between hard and soft failures. When a single table import fails due to an unexpected data type, you do not want the entire job to abort. Flag the offending record and continue. At a manufacturing client, we surfaced partial failures in a Splunk dashboard that stewards monitored daily. Ninety percent of issues were resolved without engineering involvement.

Transactionality is another consideration. The REST API offers transactional endpoints for certain operations, but extensive lineage imports may require multi-step transactions. If partial writes leave the catalog in an inconsistent state, schedule a cleanup task or maintain a checksum to detect divergence.

Lastly, rehearse disaster scenarios. Pull the network plug on a staging environment and watch the recovery process. You will uncover brittle assumptions before they bite you in production.

Real-Time versus Batch: Making the Right Call

I am often asked whether metadata synchronization must be instantaneous. The answer depends on your use case.

Real-time integration shines when data structures change frequently and downstream decisions depend on up-to-the-minute accuracy. An example is a streaming fraud platform where new Kafka topics emerge as microservices spin up. If lineage diagrams lag behind, incident responders cannot trace anomalies quickly enough.

However, real-time comes at a cost. Continuous polling or

streaming connections tax CPU, memory, and network bandwidth. They also increase the risk of cascading failures; a hiccup in one system can propagate instantly across the data estate.

Batch integration—nightly, hourly, or even weekly—suits environments where schemas are stable or where human review gates every change. A quarterly regulatory report does not require second-by-second updates. Batch jobs are easier to monitor, and windowed processing allows for heavy transformations without impacting production.

A hybrid approach often prevails. You may choose to push critical lineage updates immediately while loading descriptive attributes in bulk. Document the policy so stakeholders know what freshness to expect.

Deep Dive into Common Integration Scenarios

Let's examine a few scenarios I encounter repeatedly.

First, ingesting data warehouse metadata. Suppose you use Snowflake. Collibra Connect provides a connector that queries the INFORMATION_SCHEMA views, maps tables, columns, and constraints to your meta model, and enriches them with usage statistics. You might schedule the job nightly, but if your development teams create dozens of transient tables each day, a delta option captures only changes since the last run, reducing load.

Second, synchronizing BI reports. Tools like Tableau or Power BI embed business logic in calculated fields, parameters, and data sources. Extracting that metadata is crucial for lineage. Collibra's out-of-the-box connectors crawl server APIs, pull workbook definitions, and map them onto report asset types. One nuance I have learned is to capture user permissions as well. When a sensitive metric is exposed in a dashboard, the governance team must know who can see it.

Third, integrating data quality results. Let's say you rely on Informatica Data Quality. After each profiling run, quality scores should feed back into Collibra, triggering rules or alerts when thresholds dip. Through Connect, you can pull scorecards, join them with the relevant data asset codes, and update quality dimensions in near-real-time. This feedback loop creates a single pane of glass where stewards, analysts, and executives see not only the catalog but also the health of each asset.

Fourth, pushing access approvals downstream. You might craft a workflow where a user requests access to a dataset within Collibra. Upon approval, the workflow calls an IAM system's API to grant the requisite role in BigQuery. The key is idempotency; if an approval is revoked, the same integration should strip the role. Dual-write patterns can lead to drift, so maintain a source-of-truth flag in Collibra and reconcile nightly.

Fifth, capturing machine-learning artifact metadata. Model registries such as MLflow expose REST endpoints. By ingesting model names, versions, feature sets, and performance metrics, you extend governance to the AI realm. I once worked with a media company whose recommendation engine decayed silently because a retraining process failed. After integrating the registry, stewards set alerts on model staleness, ensuring timely retraining.

Metadata Transformation and Mapping

Rarely does source metadata fit your meta model perfectly. Transformation logic becomes the unsung hero.

For syntactic harmonization, you might convert column names to lowercase or strip special characters. It sounds trivial until you realize that PostgreSQL quotes identifiers whereas Redshift does not, leading to mismatches. Standardizing early avoids duplicates.

Semantic harmonization is harder. One system may call a field "Customer ID," another "Client Number." If both land in Collibra as separate attributes, you lose the unified view. I advocate for a business glossary that defines canonical terms, then map variations through alias relationships. During ingest, a lookup table aligns incoming labels to glossary terms.

You will also decide how to handle optional attributes. Suppose Oracle supplies column nullability, but MySQL does not. Should you default to nullable, leave the field blank, or infer from constraints? Make the rule explicit and document it so analysts know the level of confidence.

Data type mapping can be treacherous. Some systems support complex types like VARIANT or STRUCT that do not translate to simple strings or integers. Flattening may erase nuance, while serialization might inflate storage. Evaluate downstream use cases; if analysts only need a human-readable description, flattening suffices. If automated lineage analysis will parse query plans, preserve rich types.

Managing Versions and Change History

Metadata changes continuously, and capturing history is vital. Collibra stores versions implicitly by timestamping updates, but integration logic should carry meaningful context.

One approach is to embed version identifiers from source systems. For example, ETL tools often stamp job runs with a build number. When ingesting lineage, attach that number as an attribute on the Lineage Model asset. Later, if a data quality issue is traced to build 453, you can filter lineage views accordingly.

Another tactic is snapshotting. Take a full export monthly and retain it in an archival domain. Analysts can compare snapshots to see how schema complexity evolves over time. A CPG company used this to justify decommissioning old staging tables, saving thousands in cloud storage.

Be mindful of storage bloat. A healthcare provider once stored every daily snapshot, accumulating hundreds of millions of historical assets. Search slowed to a crawl. We shifted to a delta strategy, keeping only change logs and regenerating historical views on demand.

Workflows can help. Trigger a change-review process when critical attributes change, like PII flags or retention periods. Integration code publishes the change; stewards approve or reject; Collibra logs the decision. This provides an auditable trail for regulators.

Governing the Integrations Themselves

It is tempting to view integrations as purely technical, but they deserve governance, too. Treat each connector as a governed asset, with an owner, lifecycle state, SLAs, and documentation.

I once joined a project where the original integration developer had left. No one knew which cron jobs still mattered. We cataloged each integration, assigned support contacts, and tracked health metrics. During an incident, on-call staff could see which integrations were impacted and notify stakeholders proactively.

Regular reviews prevent rot. Schedule quarterly health checks to verify credentials, evaluate job duration, and retire unused connectors. You can even use Collibra itself to track integration metadata—talk about meta governance.

Case Study: FinBank's Real-Time Lineage

FinBank, a multinational bank, faced pressure from regulators to demonstrate end-to-end traceability of risk reports. Their architecture spanned Teradata, Hadoop, Informatica, and MicroStrategy. Manual lineage diagrams took weeks to compile, and discrepancies undermined credibility.

We began by cataloging systems and prioritizing those feeding Basel III reports. Collibra Connect harvested schemas nightly while the lineage harvester parsed Informatica mappings. For MicroStrategy, we leveraged a custom REST integration to extract report definitions and user permissions.

The breakthrough came when we enabled real-time change capture on Informatica. Each time a developer published a mapping, a hook fired an event to a Kafka topic. A Python microservice transformed the payload and called Collibra's API within seconds. Auditors could launch a report, drill to the source field, and view the mapping version and publication timestamp instantly.

Performance tuning was critical. Initial tests overwhelmed Collibra's write API. We implemented a queue and rate-limited inserts. Meanwhile, Collibra's search index was configured for near-real-time but not immediate refresh. We accepted a thirty-second lag, still well within regulatory tolerance.

During the next audit, FinBank demonstrated lineage in a live demo. The regulator's jaw drop was priceless, and the bank avoided a multimillion-dollar fine.

Case Study: GlobalRetail's Cloud Migration

GlobalRetail migrated from on-premise Oracle to Google BigQuery. They used the move as an opportunity to reboot data governance. The challenge was reconciling old and new metadata while maintaining reporting continuity.

We designed a phased integration. Oracle schemas were ingested via JDBC through Collibra Connect. BigQuery metadata flowed in using Google's API. For a period, both systems coexisted, so we tagged assets with a "Source Platform" attribute and built lineage across them.

An ETL scheduler in Airflow orchestrated data movement. We exposed Airflow DAG metadata through a custom Python connector. This allowed trustees to trace a KPI from a Looker dashboard back through Airflow tasks to either Oracle or BigQuery tables.

As stages completed, Oracle domains were marked "Retired," and workflows triggered stewards to validate BigQuery replacements.

After six months, Oracle connectors were disabled, documentation archived, and search facets filtered retired assets by default.

The integration layer made the migration transparent for analysts. They accessed a single Collibra portal throughout, regardless of backend changes.

Case Study: HealthLife's Data Quality Feedback Loop

HealthLife Insurance wanted to reduce claim processing errors. They deployed Talend Data Quality to catch anomalies but stewardship remained reactive. We integrated Talend results into Collibra.

After each Talend job, a post-processing script summarized record counts, error rates, and rule violations, then posted to Collibra via the REST API. Assets representing source feeds displayed red, yellow, or green statuses. Workflows auto-assigned remediation tasks to feed owners.

Within three months, error resolution time dropped by forty percent. The integration did not merely visualize issues; it mobilized people. HealthLife extended the pattern to machine-learning feature stores, ensuring high-quality inputs for predictive models.

Testing and Validation

Integration testing must span functional, performance, and

security dimensions. In my practice, we spin up a dedicated Collibra staging environment and clone production meta models. Data masking ensures no sensitive fields leak. For functional tests, we feed controlled inputs with edge cases—long object names, special characters, unexpected types—and verify correct mapping.

Performance tests simulate production volume plus a safety margin. We monitor API latency, database connections, and heap utilization. When a memory leak surfaced in a custom Java client, early stress tests prevented a nasty production outage.

Security validation encompasses penetration tests, credential audits, and role reviews. A common weakness is over-broad API tokens. We create tokens scoped to specific endpoints and verify operations fail gracefully when unauthorized.

User acceptance completes the cycle. Stewards and analysts explore lineage diagrams, glossary entries, and quality dashboards, confirming that the integrated metadata answers their questions. Their feedback often reveals subtle semantic misalignments that automated tests miss.

Maintaining and Evolving Integrations

Your data ecosystem will evolve—cloud migrations, application upgrades, reorganizations. Successful teams treat integrations as living entities.

Implement semantic versioning for connector code. When a breaking change occurs, increment the major version and run old and new connectors in parallel until consumers switch. Document deprecation timelines clearly.

Leverage feature flags. A flag allows you to enable a new mapping logic for a subset of domains, gather feedback, then roll out broadly. If issues arise, you can revert quickly.

Stay abreast of vendor roadmaps. When Tableau changed its REST API authentication model, a client who monitored beta releases refactored early and avoided downtime. Join vendor communities, subscribe to release notes, and allocate capacity for proactive upgrades.

Periodic refactoring keeps technical debt at bay. As your meta model matures, mappings that once required custom transformations may fit native attributes. Simplify code accordingly.

Cultivate cross-functional ownership. Integration developers, platform engineers, and data stewards must communicate. A weekly stand-up where issues are surfaced and prioritized prevents silent failures from festering.

Human Factors and Organizational Alignment

The most sophisticated integration architecture fails if people do not trust or use the metadata. Early in my career I built a real-time lineage solution that executives hailed as groundbreaking. Six months later usage metrics revealed decline. We discovered that analysts doubted the completeness of lineage because one key reporting system remained disconnected.

Communicate scope and limitations honestly. If lineage covers seventy percent of flows, label the remaining thirty percent as "In progress." Provide a feedback mechanism for users to flag gaps.

Celebrate integration milestones. A manufacturing firm held a "Lineage Goes Live" demo with popcorn in the break room. Fun aside, it cemented the value of the project and encouraged adoption.

Train stakeholders on new capabilities. When quality scores surfaced in Collibra, stewards needed to learn how to interpret and act on them. We ran interactive workshops where participants practiced resolving data issues end-to-end.

Recognize ownership. Assigning data owners is straightforward; assigning integration owners is less obvious. Make it explicit in RACI charts. During an outage, confusion over responsibility can prolong downtime.

Finally, secure executive sponsorship. Integration work often lies beneath the surface, but it underpins visible outcomes like faster analytics or compliance wins. Executives who grasp that linkage will defend budgets when competing priorities arise.

Measuring Integration Success

Metrics must tie to business value. On a previous project we tracked API call counts, but that number alone meant little. We shifted to metrics like time-to-catalog for new datasets, lineage coverage percentage, and reduction in duplicate data purchases. These resonated with leadership.

Delta between data quality issue detection and resolution is another powerful KPI. Integrations that loop quality findings back into Collibra often halve that time.

User satisfaction surveys indicated confidence in metadata accuracy. Before integrations, confidence averaged six out of ten. After six months, it climbed to eight.

Audit findings offer hard proof. FinBank's zero-finding audit after real-time lineage integration was compelling.

Finally, monitor platform health—API error rates, job duration, and search latency. Improvements here reflect technical excellence that supports user experience.

Conclusion: Laying the Tracks for Change Management

We began this chapter by recognizing that Collibra, without integration, is an elegant but isolated palace. By weaving it into the connective tissue of your data ecosystem, you transform governance from a passive repository to an active nerve center. We covered strategy, security, performance, error handling, real-time versus batch, and human alignment, backed by war stories from banking, retail, and healthcare.

Yet, technology alone does not guarantee adoption. In the next chapter we will shift focus to change management and user adoption strategies. You will learn how to roll out these integrated capabilities, train stakeholders, and create a culture where governed data is the default operating mode rather than an afterthought. Integration lays the tracks; change management drives the train. Let's board that journey together.

Chapter 11 Key Terms

Integration: Linking Collibra with other systems such as ETL, BI, or data-quality tools.

API Connector: A pre-built integration component that exchanges metadata automatically.

Data Lineage Harvester: A tool that extracts and imports technical lineage into Collibra.

Error Handling: The strategy for detecting and resolving integration failures.

Monitoring: Continuous observation of system performance and data synchronization.

Metadata Exchange: Two-way communication of asset information between systems.

Snowflake: A cloud data-warehouse platform often integrated with Collibra.

ETL (Extract, Transform, Load): The process of moving and shaping data between systems.

Business Intelligence (BI): Analytics technologies used to visualize and interpret data.

12

Change Management And User Adoption Strategies

Connecting the Dots: From Integration to People

In the previous chapter you and I spent time plumbing Collibra into the rest of your data ecosystem—wiring APIs, mapping metadata, and testing that reassuring moment when the lineage diagrams finally light up end-to-end. That work was essential, but it was still mainly about servers, scripts, and systems. Now the spotlight swings onto the true wildcard in any data-governance initiative: people. Your Collibra environment can hum with flawless technical integrations, yet if stewards continue to cling to spreadsheets and analysts treat the data catalog like a dusty filing cabinet, the business value we promised won't materialize.

Change management and user adoption, therefore, are not side projects that happen "once the platform is live." They are the main event. In this chapter I will walk you through the mindsets, methods, and practical experiences I have gathered helping dozens of organizations turn Collibra from "yet another tool" into a daily habit that shapes decisions. I will share the mistakes I made early on—like scheduling lunch-and-learns nobody attended—and the small victories that snowballed into enterprise-wide momentum. When we reach the final pages you will have a repeatable approach to cultivate adoption that feels natural rather than forced, so you can measure and celebrate the impact in Chapter 13.

Why Technology Alone Fails

In my first consulting engagement a global insurer spent close to a million dollars licensing Collibra and funding the integration work. Six months later every demo looked fantastic, but when the auditors asked the underwriting division to show data quality rules, the team exported a PDF from a home-grown system and ignored Collibra altogether. The project sponsor called me into her office, frustration plastered across her face. "Why did no one use the thing we built?"

The answer was not hidden in a failed technical configuration. It was cultural gravity. Underwriters were comfortable with legacy processes that had survived countless mergers. They saw the new platform as extra clicks without extra credit. Put differently, we had installed software but never earned mindshare.

Most organizations repeat this story in some form. Spending

patterns skew heavily toward technology because capital budgets feel more tangible than the soft science of change. Yet the Standish Group's CHAOS research consistently attributes over half of project failures to people issues: unclear vision, lack of executive support, low engagement, and resistance to change. When you recognize that data governance, by definition, asks people to alter how they name, define, and steward data, the emphasis on change management stops feeling optional and becomes the linchpin of success.

The Psychology of Data Governance Adoption

Before sketching timelines and training curricula, you need to understand the emotional journey your stakeholders will take. I like to borrow from Elisabeth Kübler-Ross's change curve. Even if originally conceived for grief, its stages—denial, frustration, depression, experiment, decision, integration—map uncannily well to how teams respond when Collibra arrives.

At first many deny the need. "We already have naming conventions in our data warehouse." Then frustration surfaces as old shortcuts disappear. "Why do I need to open Collibra to request access when an email used to work?" Some users slump into apathy, but others begin experimenting. They click around, discover the business glossary search actually saves them time, and gradually decide the new way is worth it. Eventually the catalog becomes invisible, woven into daily routines.

Your job is to shepherd as many people as possible through the early, painful stages quickly, so they reach experiment and integration before budget patience wears thin. The tools of that shepherding craft are vision, leadership alignment, communication, training, incentives, and social proof. We will now unpack each.

Crafting a Compelling Change Narrative

Every successful adoption journey starts with a story that resonates personally. Telling people "Collibra will improve data quality" feels abstract; telling them "you will spend sixty percent less time reconciling whose sales numbers are correct by next quarter" hits closer to home.

Begin by articulating a concise vision that ties directly to business outcomes. When I worked with a Scandinavian telecom, we reframed the governance narrative from compliance to customer experience. We spoke about activating Collibra so that any agent could instantly know a subscriber's entitlements, reducing call handling time and churn. That story secured frontline engagement far faster than a lecture on metadata stewardship.

Your narrative must also acknowledge the past. Avoid blaming current practices. Instead, position Collibra as the natural evolution of an already hardworking culture. One banking client used the phrase "honoring our operational heritage while modernizing for digital finance." Employees appreciated the nod to legacy systems they had nurtured for decades, making them more willing to embrace the new.

Sponsorship and Leadership Alignment

Stories alone cannot overcome structural hierarchy. Employees watch where leaders allocate attention. If the executive committee champions Collibra only during kickoff and then goes quiet afterward, mid-level managers receive the implicit message that adoption is optional.

I advise forming a sponsorship spine. At the top sits an executive sponsor—someone who owns a business outcome tied to data, not just the CIO. Below them a network of departmental sponsors translates the vision into domain-specific language. The finance sponsor speaks about accelerated close cycles, the marketing sponsor emphasizes campaign attribution clarity, and so on.

The most effective sponsors model behavior by logging into Collibra during steering meetings, reviewing issues, and praising teams that update metadata. I once watched a retail CEO start her quarterly town hall by searching for "net promoter score" in Collibra and showing how she traced lineage to in-store POS systems. That single act did more for adoption than three months of posters.

Creating leadership alignment also involves addressing competing initiatives. If a parallel program like ERP transformation is hogging attention, negotiate explicit integration points and shared metrics. Overlapping goals convert competition into collaboration, ensuring Collibra is viewed as complementary rather than noise.

Assessing the Organizational Landscape

Before you chart interventions, you need a baseline. I conduct a simple readiness assessment along three dimensions: culture, capability, and capacity. Culture examines attitudes toward change and data governance. Capability assesses skills—how many stewards, data engineers, and analysts already know Collibra or similar tools. Capacity considers bandwidth; during fiscal year end or product launches, adoption efforts stall because people are overloaded.

Gather insights through interviews, pulse surveys, and shadowing sessions. When I analyzed a pharmaceutical company's research division, interviews revealed scientists saw metadata entry as administrative overhead threatening publication deadlines. That insight informed our adoption plan: we embedded data librarians inside research teams to handle cataloging, enabling scientists to focus on experimentation while still benefiting from governance outcomes.

Document pain points, language preferences, and success metrics each group values. Adoption messaging for risk officers revolves around regulatory traceability, whereas product managers respond to faster feature delivery. The more granular your understanding, the more precisely you can tailor interventions.

Designing Your Multi-Layered Communication Plan

Communication in change management is often reduced to mass emails, a strategy doomed to drown in inbox clutter. Instead, treat communication as an evolving conversation delivered through multiple channels–town halls, intranet articles, instant-messaging snippets, dashboard banners inside Collibra itself.

Start with an announcement that marries vision to individual benefit, then layer in progress updates. I prefer a drumbeat rhythm: a brief update every two weeks and a deeper milestone review monthly. Shorter cycles keep momentum alive and allow rapid myth-busting. For example, when false rumors spread that Collibra would replace data engineers with AI, we issued a clarifying video the same week, preserving trust.

Language matters enormously. Governance jargon alienates business users. Replace "semantic consistency across heterogeneous data landscapes" with "everyone speaks the same numbers." If your organization spans geographies, translate messages into local languages and include region-specific case examples.

Equally important is listening. Establish feedback loops: open office hours, a chat channel monitored by the adoption team, or embedded surveys within Collibra. When users see their concerns acknowledged and features adjusted accordingly, engagement skyrockets.

Building Competency: Training, Coaching, and Communities of Practice

Most resistance evaporates once people feel competent. A one-size-fits-all training deck rarely suffices because stewardship, consuming, and architecting data require different skill sets. I recommend a blended learning pathway.

Start with role-based onboarding. Stewards attend workshops on asset creation, certification workflows, and policy attestation. Analysts learn catalog search shortcuts and lineage visualizations. Executives receive dashboard-style overviews on KPI governance. Each workshop includes hands-on exercises using real organizational data. Generic sample datasets undermine credibility; people want to see their world reflected on screen.

After initial training, provide on-demand resources—video snippets, quick-reference guides, and an internal knowledge base. These micro-learning assets work because adoption challenges often arise in the moment of need rather than scheduled sessions.

Coaching complements formal training. Assign power users or data champions who devote part of their time to peer support. At a Canadian energy firm we created a "Collibra Corner" in the office cafeteria every Wednesday. Employees could drop by with questions, and the champion resolved them live. Adoption metrics rose noticeably in departments that frequented the corner.

Communities of practice serve as the long-term scaffolding for competency. They bring together users across departments to share tips, patterns, and war stories. When the finance community demonstrated how they automated policy-triggered Jira tickets from Collibra, the idea spread to HR and logistics, magnifying platform value. Regular showcases and hackathons foster a spirit of ownership that no external consultant can replicate.

Early Wins and Social Proof: The Reactor Case Story

Theory is useful, but tangible success is persuasive. Let me share the Reactor case, a mid-market manufacturing firm that turned skeptics into advocates within three months.

Reactor's biggest pain point was part master data duplication across ERP and PLM systems. Engineers regularly submitted change requests that collided downstream, causing costly rework. We targeted this use case for an early win.

First, we configured Collibra to surface duplicate part numbers automatically and routed stewardship tasks to the responsible engineer. Instead of sending an email blast about the new feature, we invited a handful of vocal skeptics to pilot it. Within two weeks one senior engineer discovered duplicates worth $180,000 in scrapped material. He presented the finding at the next divisional meeting, citing Collibra as his "new favorite tool." That spontaneous endorsement spread faster than any official communication.

We then packaged similar success stories into short intranet posts titled "Collibra Saves the Day," attaching cost savings figures. As the anecdotes accumulated, adoption moved from novelty to necessity. By month three the engineering group reached eighty-four percent active-user rates, far exceeding initial targets.

The moral is simple: pick a pain point that matters financially or emotionally, solve it visibly, and let satisfied users become your megaphones.

Overcoming Resistance: Tactics for Different Personas

Resistance rarely announces itself plainly. It hides behind polite excuses like "We're too busy" or "The tool looks interesting but maybe next quarter." Your response must vary by persona.

For senior managers hesitant to commit resources, underscore strategic alignment and competitive risk. I once convinced a retail CFO by demonstrating on live data how inconsistent margin definitions inflated profitability forecasts by five percent, jeopardizing investor confidence. Seeing the exposure in real time jolted him into action.

Middle managers often fear disruptive workload. Offer them coverage: temporary interns to assist with data curation, or automation scripts that import metadata so their teams are not saddled with manual entry. When a public-sector agency introduced automated lineage from Informatica, stewards reclaimed eight hours a week, flipping their outlook from hostility to gratitude.

Frontline employees crave recognition. Tie Collibra adoption to performance reviews or highlight champions during town halls. I recall a healthcare data analyst who hesitated to catalog datasets because she thought it was outside her job scope. After the CIO publicly applauded her contribution, she not only continued cataloging but also mentored peers.

Technical architects sometimes worry about security or integration complexity. Involve them early in design workshops and pilot phases so they feel ownership. Their endorsement often sways broader IT teams who respect architectural authority.

Throughout, keep empathy high. Resistance reflects legitimate concerns about competence, workload, or job security. Address those root fears rather than labeling opponents as obstructionists.

Embedding Collibra into Daily Routines

True adoption happens when the platform becomes the path of least resistance. To achieve this, integrate Collibra into existing workflows rather than creating a parallel universe.

At a large credit-card company we embedded a Collibra widget directly into the Tableau dashboard header. Analysts exploring visualizations could click a dataset and instantly open its glossary article. By shortening context-switching friction to a single click, we turned passive catalog awareness into active usage.

Email notifications from workflows should include deep links to the exact task, reducing navigation steps. When stewards receive a "certify data set" prompt, they land precisely on the certification page, not Collibra's generic homepage.

APIs enable even tighter coupling. A logistics company created a Slack bot that, upon typing "data orders," queried Collibra for the canonical order definitions and posted them back in channel.

Employees never consciously used Collibra, yet adoption metrics soared because the platform hid behind the bot.

Measuring embedment involves tracking not just logins but transactions initiated by external systems. Over time, aim for a state where more than half of Collibra interactions originate from tools users already rely on. That is the clearest sign governance has woven itself into organizational fabric.

Incentives, Recognition, and the Culture Shift

Culture changes when behaviors are reinforced publicly and consistently. Incentives need not be monetary. At an aerospace manufacturer we instituted a "Golden Steward" badge displayed on Collibra profiles of users who achieved ninety-five percent task completion. The badge became a status symbol, sparking friendly competition across teams.

Performance management systems offer formal reinforcement. Linking governance contributions to annual reviews signals leadership commitment. One insurer updated its competency framework to include "data citizenship," awarding top ratings to employees who championed Collibra adoption. Within a year the platform moved from niche to mainstream as everyone realized it could influence bonuses.

Storytelling also drives cultural shift. Celebrate not only big wins but the everyday acts of discipline—like a marketing associate who corrects a glossary term before launching a campaign. Share these micro-stories on digital signage or newsletters, reinforcing the message that small behaviors accumulate into strategic advantage.

Finally, embed Collibra language in corporate vocabulary. Replace "check the spreadsheet" with "consult the catalog" during meetings. The more casually people refer to the platform, the deeper the cultural imprint.

Monitoring Pulse and Course-Correcting

Change is neither linear nor predictable. Monitor adoption continually and be ready to pivot. Collibra provides out-of-the-box usage statistics, but numbers alone only tell half the story. Qualitative insights from surveys, focus groups, and anecdotal observations reveal why metrics trend up or down.

When I saw active users plateau at a media company, we conducted "barrier interviews." We discovered that the search feature performed poorly for non-English keywords commonly used by international reporters. Addressing this linguistic gap reignited adoption. Had we relied solely on login counts, we might have misinterpreted the plateau as inevitable saturation.

Set checkpoints—perhaps every six weeks—where the adoption team reviews both quantitative and qualitative data, identifies impediments, and deploys corrective actions. Treat the process like agile sprints, iterating on communication tactics, training materials, or technical improvements.

Transparency about these adjustments fosters trust. When users see their feedback reflected in platform updates or policy tweaks, they feel valued and remain engaged.

Sustainability Through Continuous Engagement

The honeymoon period of a new tool eventually fades. To sustain momentum, evolve your engagement model from project-led to community-led. Communities of practice, champion networks, and self-service analytics portals become the drivers while central governance teams shift to facilitators.

Introduce advanced use cases—data quality dashboards, AI-assisted lineage suggestions—that keep the platform fresh. Rotate stewardship roles to prevent burnout and inject new perspectives. Encourage academic partnerships or hackathons to explore innovative applications of Collibra metadata.

Institutionalize periodic health checks. Much like physical wellness exams, these reviews assess metadata completeness, workflow throughput, and user satisfaction. Publish the findings, celebrate the healthy areas, and set improvement targets for lagging domains.

Remember sustainability also depends on funding. Secure operational budgets rather than relying solely on project funds. Governance is a perpetual discipline, and so is the user-adoption engine that underpins it.

Closing Thoughts and the Road to Measurement

By now you should appreciate that change management is less about coaxing people to "use a tool" and more about orchestrating a symphony of vision, leadership, communication, capability, and cultural reinforcement. If you invest in these levers with the same rigor you applied to integrating data pipelines, Collibra will graduate from system to habit, from habit to reflex.

Of course, prudent leaders still ask, "How will we know all this effort is paying off?" That question sets the stage for our next chapter.

We will move from the qualitative art of persuasion to the quantitative science of measurement. Together we will define Key Performance Indicators, design dashboards, and build the evidence base that proves your data governance program is not only popular but powerful. I will meet you there.

Chapter 12 Key Terms

User Adoption: The extent to which end users effectively embrace and use new systems.

Change Resistance: Human or organizational reluctance to modify established routines.

Training Plan: A structured approach to developing user competence in Collibra.

Awareness Campaign: Communication designed to inform and excite stakeholders about the program.

Executive Sponsorship: Visible endorsement and support from senior leadership.

Recognition Strategy: Formal acknowledgment of individuals who contribute to adoption success.

Cultural Inertia: The tendency of organizations to revert to familiar but outdated behaviors.

Feedback Loop: A mechanism for collecting user input and improving engagement.

13

Measuring Success And Kpi Development

Transitioning from Adoption to Proof

In the previous chapter you and I walked through the people side of the rollout, the town-hall announcements, the lunch-and-learn sessions, the quiet coaching moments at individual desks. By now your early adopters have clicked around in Collibra, cataloged their first data assets, perhaps triggered a workflow or two, and the organization is beginning to whisper the new governance vocabulary. This is the point where curiosity alone no longer moves the program forward. Budgets tighten, executives grow restless, and the internal skeptic in every stakeholder leans forward with the inevitable question: "So, what have we actually achieved?"

If there is a single truth, I have learned from running governance programs on four different continents, it is that good intentions without proof eventually wither. People do not invest year over year in feel-good stories; they invest in measurable value. Chapter 13 is therefore the moment we shift from evangelists to empiricists. Together we will build the measurement framework that turns Collibra from a promising tool into an engine that continuously demonstrates tangible business benefit.

Why Measurement Matters to Every Persona

When I first introduced a KPI scorecard to a team of data stewards in a European insurance firm, an experienced steward raised his hand and said, "We know why KPIs matter to executives, but why should we care? We are already overloaded with data quality tasks." His question was honest and representative of many teams. The answer sits in an unexpected corner: professional pride.

For data owners, seeing the percentage of critical data elements with assigned stewardship climb from thirty to eighty feels like watching a garden bloom after months of unseen soil work. For business users, a reduction in time spent searching for lineage can translate into reclaimed hours during a high-stakes quarter-end closing. Even for the most technical engineer deep in the metadata integration layer, performance metrics validate that the pipelines they built are not mere academic exercises but improvements that shorten delivery cycles for the entire company.

Measurement, then, becomes the common language across personas. It aligns the board member seeking strategic advantage, the analyst chasing trusted numbers, and the steward nurturing semantic accuracy. Everyone can disagree about priorities in a steering committee, yet nobody argues with an agreed-upon metric trending in the right direction.

Finding Your North Star Metric

Software start-ups talk about a North Star metric that captures the essence of customer value. In governance we need the same clarity, even though the landscape feels more complex. I encourage every organization to pick one overarching metric that is simple enough to remember, visible enough to track weekly, and business-oriented enough that a non-technical executive nods in recognition.

At a pharmaceutical client I guided, we landed on "approved data definitions for all key terms referenced in regulatory filings." It sounds almost mundane, but the company's core risk lay in misinterpretation of drug trial results. By honing in on the existence and quality of approved definitions, we connected Collibra's workflow automation directly to faster, safer submissions to the FDA and EMA. The North Star did not negate the need for other KPIs; it simply acted as the lighthouse. Whenever we debated backlog prioritization, we asked, "Will this sprint move the approved definitions percentage upward?" That single question reduced stakeholder noise by half.

You, too, will feel pressure to define ten, twenty, even forty KPIs out of the gate. Resist. Craft one North Star first, socialize it broadly, observe how it resonates, and then add supporting measures in a deliberate cascade.

Building a KPI Tree that Mirrors the Governance Operating Model

Imagine your operating model from Chapter Four as a hierarchy of responsibilities: executive sponsors at the top, data councils, domain owners, stewards, custodians, and technology enablers. A good KPI framework mirrors that tree. I like to sketch it out on a whiteboard: the North Star perched at the apex, then branch down into contributor KPIs that each role can influence.

For example, suppose the North Star is "time to trusted data for analytics use cases." Underneath, the data stewardship branch might own "percentage of assets with validated lineage," the quality branch might own "critical data elements passing all automated checks," while the integration branch owns "refresh latency of metadata imports." Each child KPI inherits part of the variance of the parent. If your lineage KPI lags, you already know which section of the operating model requires coaching or resource adjustment.

By architecting the KPI tree to reflect governance roles, you avoid the classic pitfall of throwing aggregate metrics onto dashboards and then shrugging when nobody knows who is supposed to act. Every metric becomes a call to a specific group, a to-do rather than a vanity statistic.

Data Availability and the Collibra Reporting Landscape

Collibra quietly collects a wealth of operational data every time you click a button, approve a workflow, or edit an attribute. Much of that information lives in the Collibra Data Governance Center database, and you can surface it through the out-of-the-box dashboards in Collibra Insights, or access it via the Reporting Data Layer.

Yet merely opening Insights is like walking into an enormous natural history museum without a map. Specimens abound, but they appear random until curators weave a storyline. I learned this lesson the hard way during an early deployment when I presented executives with a dashboard that included asset counts, community counts, workflow task durations, and login frequencies all on one screen. The feedback was predictable: "What do we look at first, and why should we care?"

Before you pull the first chart, trace each KPI back to the raw metadata source: schema, community, asset type, workflow table, or lineage table. Then confirm that the data refresh cycle matches the granularity you need. I once spent two weeks troubleshooting why a data quality score remained static only to discover that the integration updating the governing dataset ran monthly while the dashboard refreshed nightly. Synchronizing cadence matters as much as the metric itself.

Designing Dashboards that Tell a Story

Humans think in narratives more easily than in grids. When you design a KPI dashboard, imagine you are preparing slides for a board meeting where you have exactly three minutes before someone's phone buzzes. Your aim is a visual journey: current state, movement compared with last period, and a clear implication.

In practice, this means placing the North Star front and center, using color to show variance against target, and layering supporting KPIs below in logical order. At a consumer goods company, we designed a "sprint runway" dashboard: top banner with overall governance maturity score as the North Star, then successive bands for data quality, stewardship engagement, workflow throughput, and platform adoption. Executives learned to read it like the morning weather report. "Green across stewardship, amber on quality; we know our next area of focus."

Remember to use plain English labels on charts. A beautifully calculated metric loses impact when the caption reads "XGOV_QUAL_PCT_CURR.Q4" instead of "Percentage of critical elements passing quality rules." Your goal is to reduce mental translation overhead so the viewer concentrates on decision making, not decoding.

Moving from Lagging to Leading Indicators

Most teams start with lagging indicators because they are easy to measure: number of assets catalogued, count of steward assignments, percentage of workflows completed. These tell you what has already happened, but they rarely predict the future. To manage a program proactively, you need leading indicators that signal upcoming risk or opportunity.

One of my favorite leading indicators is “average time between issue creation and first steward response.” If this metric begins to slide from two days to five, you do not yet feel the downstream pain, but you know morale and data quality will suffer soon. Another is “ratio of certified data sets to total sets used in production dashboards.” Improving that ratio today prevents tomorrow’s flood of support tickets questioning data accuracy.

Collibra makes leading indicators feasible because of its real-time workflow audit logs. With a simple SQL view over the workflow history tables, you can calculate step durations, identify bottlenecks, and flag tasks that breach SLA before they snowball into non-compliance events.

Establishing Baselines and Setting Targets

A common anxiety surfaces during KPI workshops: “We’ve never measured this before, how do we know what good looks like?”

The answer is to start with a baseline period rather than a benchmark. Measure without judgment for four to six weeks. Observe natural variability. Then set improvement targets based on percentile shifts rather than arbitrary industry averages.

At a North American retailer we tracked the baseline of "time to approve business definition." The first cut averaged twelve days. The team's instinct was to declare a two-day target, but a deeper look revealed legal review alone took five days due to regulatory constraints. We settled on an eight-day target, of which three days were variable discretionary time. Six months later the metric hit five days, not by whipping the team faster but by identifying redundant approval steps. Targets based on baseline data encourage sustainable improvement rather than heroic sprints that risk burning out staff.

Automating Metric Collection inside Collibra

The magic moment in a governance program arrives when KPIs harvest themselves. No more manual spreadsheet gymnastics every Friday afternoon. Collibra's Workflow Designer, when paired with the REST API, allows you to embed metric increments inside normal user activity.

For instance, at an energy utility we modified the asset certification workflow: as soon as a steward clicked "Approve certification," the workflow posted an incremental update to a custom KPI asset called "Certification Counter." The dashboard reading from that asset updated instantly. The steward's cognitive load remained unchanged, yet the KPI tracked live progress.

If you are concerned about API quotas, remember most KPI updates involve tiny payloads. The heavier call volumes come from bulk ingestion jobs, not single counter updates.

Dealing with Data Quality Challenges in Your KPI Data

Ironically, the data that describes your governance success must itself be governed. I have watched proud teams present KPI dashboards only to face immediate questions about accuracy. To avoid that embarrassment, treat your KPI data as a first-class citizen. Assign an owner, document the lineage, and store definitions in Collibra's glossary. During a financial audit at a European bank, we discovered that two dashboards calculated "active users" differently—one by unique login ID, the other by session token. Harmonizing the definitions not only fixed the immediate confusion but also underscored the value of Collibra as the single point of truth, even about its own usage metrics.

Data quality on KPI feeds improves when you build validation steps into the ETL jobs. If a metric value suddenly deviates beyond three standard deviations from its trailing average, the pipeline can pause and alert a steward to verify. This saves the leadership meeting from dramatic spikes caused by ingestion errors.

Socializing Results and Creating a Feedback Loop

Publishing a dashboard is not enough; you need an explicit rhythm for review and action. I advocate for a tiered cadence: weekly stand-ups for operational teams, monthly forums for data councils, and quarterly updates for executives. In each meeting, begin with the trends, then drill down to root causes, then assign corrective tasks back into the agile backlog.

At one manufacturing client we replaced a static slide deck with a standing "KPI cockpit" session every Wednesday morning. Each steward arrived having already reviewed the live dashboard. Discussion time dropped by thirty percent because everyone shared the same real-time view. More importantly, action items were logged directly into JIRA tickets on the spot, closing the loop between metric insight and operational change.

Case Study: The Global Bank That Learned to Speak KPI

Allow me to share a flagship example. A global bank with operations in twenty-eight countries embarked on a Collibra rollout to tame fragmented customer data. Initial adoption looked promising, but after twelve months the program risked losing funding. The governance lead, whom I had mentored, convinced the executive committee to grant sixty days to prove value.

The team crafted a North Star: "percentage of customer records with unified identifier across retail and corporate systems." They mapped contributory KPIs down to data quality match rates, steward assignment completion, and metadata import frequency. Dashboards went live within three weeks.

Surprises emerged immediately. A particular region showed stellar stewardship but dismal match rates, pinpointing a systemic issue in one source system's data entry form. Within two weeks that form was redesigned. The match rate rose from fifty to eighty-seven percent, boosting the North Star metric by ten points.

At the sixty-day executive review, the program showcased not just improved numbers but the cause-and-effect story of how Collibra enabled pinpoint remediation. The budget was renewed for three years, with explicit KPI targets written into the governance charter. The bank later reported a reduction of customer onboarding time by fifteen percent, directly attributing it to data unification tracked through the KPI framework.

Personal Anecdote: The Day the Dashboard Saved My Budget Meeting

On a lighter, more personal note, I still recall a tense Friday afternoon at a telecommunications company. I was slated to defend the Collibra renewal fee to a cost-cutting finance director. Minutes before the call, I opened the latest KPI dashboard. I noticed that time to provision analytics data had dropped from nine to four days over the past quarter. Armed with that number, I reframed the conversation. Rather than starting with license costs, I began: "We saved your analysts five days every release cycle. At your blended rate, that is one point two million dollars annually." The renewal was approved in under ten minutes. Measurement did not merely support the case; it wrote the entire narrative.

Maintaining Momentum: Quarterly Reviews and Continuous Calibration

Metrics can become stale if left unchallenged. The project that seems revolutionary today might be table stakes next year. That is why I recommend a formal quarterly review of the KPI tree itself, not just the metric results. Ask whether each KPI still correlates to a strategic objective. Confirm that data sources remain reliable. Retire metrics that have reached sustained performance; add new ones that reflect emerging governance goals like data privacy or machine learning model transparency.

One global retailer swapped out "number of catalogued assets" for "coverage ratio of high-value analytics dashboards" once asset counts plateaued. This pivot kept the governance program aligned with business outcomes rather than celebrating raw volume.

When the Numbers Say You're Off Track

Sooner or later a metric will flash red and leadership will ask why.

In such moments transparency trumps bravado. Admit the issue, trace it with the same rigor you applied to success stories, and plot a remediation path. At a healthcare provider, a sudden dip in certified data sets revealed a staffing gap after a steward's resignation. By presenting the data openly, the program secured expedited hiring approval rather than suffering reputational damage. Honest metrics breed trust, which in turn breeds continued investment.

The Role of Advanced Analytics and AI in Governance KPIs

As your Collibra environment matures, you will accumulate years of workflow histories, asset changes, and quality scores. This data set is fertile ground for predictive modelling. Imagine forecasting which domains will breach data quality thresholds next quarter, or which stewardship teams are likely to fall behind due to seasonal workload spikes.

I experimented with a simple random forest model on workflow duration data for a logistics client. The model predicted seventy-two percent of potential SLA breaches two days before they occurred, giving the team time to reallocate resources. Such predictive KPIs transform governance from reactive monitoring to proactive orchestration.

Collibra's built-in APIs make it straightforward to export activity logs into a data lake where your data science team can play. Just remember to loop the predictions back into Collibra for visibility; a model left in isolation offers little value.

Preparing for Executive Readouts and Board-Level Reporting

Executive audiences demand brevity and relevance. They care less about steward response times and more about revenue protection, regulatory compliance, and strategic agility. Translate your core KPIs into those dimensions. For instance, link improved data quality scores to reduced operational risk fines, or tie faster issue resolution times to accelerated product launches.

In board meetings I use a three-slide structure. Slide one presents the North Star trend line over the last four quarters. Slide two highlights two supporting KPIs with concise explanation of drivers. Slide three outlines the next set of actions and required support. The entire segment takes under seven minutes and invariably invites engaged questions instead of glazed eyes.

Embedding KPI Thinking into Everyday Workflows

The final maturity stage arrives when individual contributors reference KPIs as naturally as they reference project deadlines. This cultural shift happens when you embed metric feedback within the tools people already use. Display the stewardship backlog health directly in the Certification workflow start page. Show data quality trending inside the lineage viewer. The less users have to hunt for performance numbers, the more they will internalize them.

One of my clients added a simple "my impact" ribbon on every steward's landing page in Collibra, summarizing how their recent approvals affected the North Star metric. Engagement soared because the platform celebrated small wins in real time.

Conclusion: Measuring to Improve, Not to Impress

If you remember only one lesson from this chapter, let it be that KPIs are instruments of improvement, not trophies. Collibra provides the raw signal; your job is to interpret, act, and refine. By selecting a clear North Star, cascading metrics through the operating model, automating collection, and maintaining an honest feedback loop, you create a governance program that justifies itself every single day. As we pivot to the next chapter, we will examine the darker corners–the common pitfalls and troubleshooting techniques that stand ready to derail even the most meticulously measured initiative. Armed with your new KPI framework, you will be better prepared to spot trouble early and steer your Collibra voyage toward lasting success.

Chapter 13 Key Terms

KPI (Key Performance Indicator): A measurable value that demonstrates progress toward a business objective.

Metric: A quantitative measure used to assess performance or compliance.

Data Usage Analytics: Tracking how users interact with governed data assets.

Transparency: Open sharing of metrics and progress to build trust.

Dashboard: A visual display summarizing governance and performance metrics.

Cycle Time: The time taken for a governance request or task to complete end-to-end.

Benchmarking: Comparing performance metrics against best practices or peers.

ROI (Return on Investment): A calculation demonstrating financial benefits relative to costs.

14

Common Pitfalls And Troubleshooting Guide

Picking Up from the Numbers

In the previous chapter I encouraged you to wrap meaningful numbers around your Collibra program. Dashboards, service-level objectives, adoption funnels, and executive scorecards all help you follow the facts rather than your intuition. As soon as you start tracking those measures, however, you will discover gaps between what you hoped to see and what actually shows up on the screen. That gap is the entrance ramp to this chapter. We are about to walk straight into the places where Collibra programs most often derail and—more important—learn how to drive them back on track before the damage becomes irreversible.

I have sat in conference rooms where optimistic timelines were written on whiteboards, only to be erased three months later when the same team found itself buried under conflicting definitions, half-finished workflows, and performance complaints. I have also worked with organizations that turned near-failures into exemplary programs

by confronting root causes early and head-on. Those lessons, collected over the last decade, form the backbone of this troubleshooting guide.

Why Pitfalls Surface Even in Well-Run Programs

Collibra implementations are deceptively complex. The user interface looks friendly, the catalog search feels familiar, and the workflow canvas appears to offer drag-and-drop simplicity. Underneath, though, each configuration choice touches policies, people, and systems you may not fully control. Most pitfalls emerge at the seams—where technology collides with culture, where speed conflicts with governance, where enthusiasm runs up against budget.

You could design the most elegant meta model in the world, yet if the data stewards who must populate it do not have dedicated time, the model remains an empty shell. You could build perfectly tuned APIs, yet if the producing systems send malformed metadata, Collibra can only ingest garbage at high speed. In other words, pitfalls rarely announce themselves as software bugs. They show up as missed expectations.

Recognizing this dynamic is liberating because it tells you where to look first when something goes wrong. Before you rewrite a workflow, ask whether the business policy behind it is still valid. Before you purchase more servers to improve performance, verify that your catalog is not bloated with obsolete assets. The point is simple: technical symptoms often mask human or process causes.

The Organizational Traps: Governance Without Authority

The most common non-technical failure I encounter is the so-called advisory council with no teeth. A company will proudly unveil a data governance board, populate it with respected leaders, give it a visionary charter, and then ask members to volunteer an hour a month. After a quarter, they discover nobody shows up, policies are delayed, and stewardship assignments languish. When Collibra finally goes live, there is no authoritative body to resolve ownership conflicts. Data sets end up with two stewards or, worse, with none at all.

I once worked with a global retailer that tried to solve this problem by adding more PowerPoint. Every month they produced beautifully formatted slides listing overdue stewardship tasks. The slide deck grew thicker, but the tasks remained stuck.

The slide deck grew thicker while the tasks remained stuck. The breakthrough came when the chief data officer tied stewardship completion to the annual performance reviews of the business line leaders. Suddenly, tasks that had been overdue for six months were finished in a week. Collibra was the same platform, but the governance body behind it had gained real authority.

The immediate troubleshooting lesson is that you must audit the mandate of every committee or steering group linked to Collibra. If the mandate is purely advisory, escalate until you secure decision rights over data definitions, quality thresholds, and allocation of stewardship resources. Without that escalation, you will burn time fixing the same ownership conflicts in every sprint.

Meta Model Missteps: Building on Shaky Ground

The meta model is your foundation. A crack you overlook on day one can later spread, warping every asset that rests on it. The most frequent meta model mistake is over-customization. Teams get excited about Collibra's flexibility and start adding asset types for every conceivable nuance: bronze data set, silver data set, gold data set, platinum data set, and so on. Three months later they realize that the classification scheme is actually a single attribute, not four distinct asset types, and they have to execute a painful migration.

Early in my consulting career I helped a financial institution that attempted to model each regulatory report as its own asset type. By the time we arrived, they had twenty-three regulatory-specific asset types that differed only by two attributes. The catalog was a labyrinth. Search results returned identical fields living under different parent assets, making data lineage almost impossible to generate. The fix involved collapsing those twenty-three asset types into one standardized Report asset with a simple drop-down attribute for regulation. It took a weekend of API scripting and a month of change management, but the search experience improved overnight.

If your users complain that they cannot find what they are looking for, examine the meta model first. Look for redundant asset types, attributes that duplicate information, or relationship types that serve no analytical purpose. Migrating may appear daunting, yet leaving the meta model in a malformed state guarantees ongoing confusion and hinders any scaling effort you plan to attempt later.

Workflow Woes: When Automation Hinders Instead of Helps

Collibra's process engine tempts every governance team to codify the perfect workflow on day one. The trouble is that most organizations do not yet understand how their future-state processes will behave at scale. They automate an untested policy and, within days, inboxes overflow with approval tasks that nobody knows how to handle. The result is a backlog that feels like a traffic jam caused by a new traffic light with the wrong timing.

A technology company I assisted built a lineage certification workflow that required three approvals for every table. In the staging environment, with a handful of assets, the workflow looked flawless. In production, faced with forty thousand tables, the approvals exploded. Hundreds of stewards received daily reminders, and because they could not keep up, the workflow never advanced past the first gate. By the end of the first week, the compliance team considered rolling back the entire implementation.

We recovered by turning that complex workflow into a two-step process: a single steward verified lineage, and a weekly sampling audit assured compliance. The automated reminders decreased, the backlog cleared, and the certification program became sustainable. The moral is straightforward: treat workflows like living organisms. Start lean, measure throughput, and add complexity only when data proves the process can handle it.

Integration Nightmares: The Metadata Gets Lost in Translation

Your Collibra implementation is only as reliable as its integration points. When the lineage tool, the data quality engine, or the business glossary in another platform sends malformed or incomplete metadata, what lands in Collibra is a distorted mirror image of reality. Troubleshooting such issues requires a detective mindset because symptoms may appear in Collibra while the root cause hides two systems away.

Consider the healthcare provider that spent six months blaming Collibra for duplicating thousands of catalog entries. We traced the issue back to the ingestion script reading from their enterprise data lake. Each time the lake processed a new daily partition, the script interpreted the partition as a brand-new data set rather than an update to an existing one. Collibra ingested faithfully, day after day, and the catalog ballooned. Fixing Collibra would not have solved anything; we had to change the parsing logic upstream.

The cure for integration nightmares is end-to-end contract testing. Every upstream system that feeds Collibra must publish a schema contract. If the contract changes, the Collibra ingestion pipeline should fail fast with a meaningful alert. You would rather have a small outage you can diagnose quickly than silent corruption that goes unnoticed for months. The moment you feel tempted to hack a workaround inside Collibra, stop and validate the data at the source.

The Performance Paradox: Catalog Sluggishness and User Frustration

Few things erode user confidence faster than a slow search experience. Collibra's underlying database is robust, but when a catalog grows to millions of assets and retains historical versions of everything, even the best infrastructure can struggle. The paradox is that performance issues often arise in the most successful programs—the ones that have ingested vast numbers of assets because adoption is high. The danger is that adoption can plummet as quickly as it grew once performance degrades.

At a multinational manufacturer, search latency climbed from two seconds to fifteen after the team imported sensor data sets from dozens of factories. Users complained, executives noticed, and the project lead feared an unexpected hardware purchase was imminent. Instead, we performed a usage analysis. It turned out that ninety-five percent of searches were limited to the three most recent months of data. Older versions were seldom accessed. By pruning obsolete versions and archiving assets untouched for more than a year, we reduced the catalog size by forty percent and restored sub-second response times without adding a single server.

Whenever performance drops, step back and ask two questions: first, has the catalog accumulated redundant or stale content; second, are versioning settings more aggressive than necessary. Collibra's retention and archival policies exist for a reason. Configuring them thoughtfully is often cheaper and faster than scaling hardware.

Security and Access Challenges: Balancing Protection and Productivity

Security policies in highly regulated industries can cripple a Collibra roll-out if they are too rigid. I have seen organizations limit catalog visibility so severely that new users could not even see asset names, only error messages. Those users concluded Collibra was broken and stopped logging in. On the opposite extreme, I encountered a startup that granted everyone full administrator privileges. A junior analyst deleted half the community hierarchy by accident, and we spent the weekend restoring from backup.

A balanced approach requires mapping security roles to business personas rather than to directory groups alone. Think through the daily tasks of a data steward, a business analyst, and an executive sponsor. Then ensure each persona has the minimum rights to perform those tasks without filling the interface with buttons they should never click. Regularly review roles and entitlements as personnel change. The task sounds tedious, but ignoring it will either stall adoption or expose you to accidental data loss. Both outcomes are avoidable with modest upfront diligence.

Adoption Stagnation: The Human Side of Failure

Technical fixes can be straightforward; human behavior rarely is. Adoption typically plateaus when the novelty wears off and the next big corporate priority steals attention. Executives expect usage graphs to keep climbing, but if middle managers do not reinforce the value of Collibra in team meetings, everyday work gravitates back to spreadsheets and shared email attachments

One pharmaceutical company I worked with experienced exactly this pattern. After an energetic launch, weekly active users climbed from zero to eight hundred in two months, then flatlined. We interviewed a sample of users and discovered they had no idea how to interpret catalog quality ratings, so they preferred the familiarity of locally stored CSV files. The remediation plan involved short video tutorials embedded directly in Collibra, showing side-by-side comparisons of approved versus unapproved data sets. Within six weeks, active usage resumed its upward trend.

The lesson is that training must evolve as the platform matures.

Early on, you teach how to log in and search. Later, you teach how to interpret quality scores and lineage diagrams. Eventually, you teach how to submit change requests and build community statistics. Treat adoption as a life cycle, not a one-off event.

Measurement Blind Spots: Data About Data That Goes Dark

In Chapter 13 we explored key performance indicators. The irony is that measurements designed to prove success can hide failure if they are not scrutinized. Suppose your primary metric is catalog growth. If the catalog swells with irrelevant assets, the metric reports success while user satisfaction plummets. Or imagine a workflow completion rate that looks stellar because users found a loophole: they skip mandatory fields, mark tasks complete, and push the workflow forward.

That exact scenario unfolded at an insurance company that tracked stewardship completion rates. The rate appeared to hit one hundred percent within deadline, which seemed miraculous—until an audit revealed stewards entered placeholder text such as "TBD" to avoid missing due dates. Real completion was closer to thirty percent. We adapted the metric by adding a quality threshold: attributes had to pass a regex validation to count as complete. Instantly, the KPI dropped sharply, and the organization finally confronted its true baseline.

The corrective action is to stress test every metric. Ask how it could be gamed, whether it measures lagging or leading behavior, and how it surfaces qualitative nuance. The moment you notice a discrepancy between what a number reports and what people experience, drill deeper. Otherwise, your dashboard becomes a comfort blanket that conceals structural failure.

Crisis Case Files: Stories From the Trenches

Stories cement theory into memory, so let me share three mini-case studies. The first involves a public energy utility that pushed a major Collibra upgrade on the same day it refreshed LDAP roles. Overnight, no one could log in. The outage lasted only four hours, yet the perception of instability lingered for months. Now that team stages upgrades in a sandbox, then executes a blue-green deployment to allow instant rollback.

The second case features an e-commerce giant that automated lineage ingestion from its data pipeline orchestrator. When engineers refactored job names to new naming standards, lineage ingestion began mapping old job identifiers to new asset entries, fragmenting the lineage graph. We wrote a translation layer so the ingest script always resolves legacy identifiers to the canonical names before creating assets. It was a small mapping table, but it saved analysts from chasing lineage ghosts.

The third story centers on a federal agency that discovered its glossary was rife with duplicate definitions–five variations of "customer," seven of "transaction," and even two of "fiscal year." The duplication stemmed from an overzealous import of legacy glossaries without deduplication. The team responded with a sprint dedicated solely to rationalization. They froze new glossary entries, convened domain experts, merged synonyms, and instituted a governance rule that any term resembling an existing concept must be linked as an alternate name, not a new entry. By the next release, glossary search went from chaotic to coherent.

These cases illustrate a common pattern: a localized decision—a scheduling oversight, a refactor, a bulk import—cascaded into systemic pain. Rapid detection and targeted remediation prevented long-term damage.

A Practical Troubleshooting Framework

When something breaks, panic clouds judgment. I advise every Collibra program to adopt a simple, repeatable framework. Step one is triage: define the blast radius. Is the issue limited to one community, one workflow, one integration, or is it platform-wide? Step two is reproduction: can you replicate the error in a non-production environment? If not, you may be looking at a transient external dependency. Step three is root cause analysis: gather logs, check recent changes, and interview users to reconstruct the timeline. Step four is resolution: implement the smallest viable fix that restores service while preventing recurrence. Step five is retrospective:

document what happened, why it happened, and how you will guard against it next time.

I follow this framework religiously because it transforms a crisis into a learning opportunity. Even if you technically fix the bug, you have not learned unless you record the conditions that allowed it. Those notes later form your institutional memory. They shorten resolution the next time a similar issue surfaces, and they prove invaluable when onboarding new team members who must absorb years of lessons in weeks.

Building a Culture That Reduces Repeat Failures

Tools and frameworks matter, yet culture is the multiplier. Organizations that treat pitfalls as blame sessions stagnate, while those that treat them as educational events accelerate. I recall a bank where every incident triggered a management hunt for the guilty. Engineers hid problems until they spiraled. Compare that to a media company where the same incident severity launched a blameless post-mortem. Engineers surfaced issues early, knowing their honesty would be rewarded with support rather than punishment.

To replicate the latter culture, establish psychological safety. Acknowledge publicly when someone spots a potential failure before it hits production. Reward teams that volunteer to own messy problems. Frame every troubleshooting session as an exploration, not a trial. When you embed those behaviors, Collibra becomes more than software; it turns into a living system that grows more robust with each challenge.

From Recovery to Resilience: Preparing for the Next Phase

Each pitfall you navigate equips you for the scaling journey that awaits in the next chapter. The same patterns—meta model drift, workflow overload, integration fragility—will resurface when you double your asset count or expand governance to a new division. The difference is that you now possess battle-tested strategies. You can spot early warning signs, mobilize triage quickly, and institutionalize the fix. Resilience is not a static state; it is a habit of continuous learning.

In the upcoming chapter we will shift our focus from firefighting to forward momentum. We will explore how to scale Collibra implementations across the enterprise, iterate on your governance operating model, and embed a culture of ongoing optimization. Think of the lessons you just absorbed as the survival kit you will carry into that next ascent.

Chapter 14 Key Terms

Over-Engineering: Adding unnecessary complexity that reduces usability or slows progress.

Technical Debt: The future cost incurred by quick fixes or shortcuts taken during implementation.

Burnout: Exhaustion caused by sustained workload without adequate rest or recognition.

Root-Cause Analysis: A method for identifying the fundamental reason behind recurring problems.

Workflow Abandonment: When users stop engaging with automated processes due to friction or confusion.

Remediation: Corrective action taken to fix governance or data-quality issues.

Post-Mortem: A structured review conducted after a failure to extract lessons learned.

Continuous Monitoring: Ongoing tracking of system health and governance compliance.

15

Scaling And Continuous Improvement

The Moment You Realize It's Working

Somewhere around the twelfth month of most Collibra programs, there is a morning when you walk into the office, open your laptop, and notice that the platform is quietly humming along without anyone nudging it. Stewards are approving definitions over their coffee, an analyst in Madrid is searching the business glossary for a term she has never seen before, and the data quality dashboard is lighting up in red and green with the rhythm of automated checks you orchestrated weeks earlier. The pilot domain you started with—maybe customer data, maybe product—has already spawned new onboarding requests from lines of business that were once skeptical. You exhale and realize that everything you have been building is, at last, driving value on its own.

That feeling is exhilarating, but it also comes with a lurking question: what now? Scaling and continuous improvement are not about maintaining the status quo; they are about transforming an early success into an enterprise-wide capability that can weather acquisitions, reorganizations, new regulations, and technology shifts you cannot yet predict. Over the next few pages I want us to explore how you make that leap from local victory to sustained, organization-spanning impact, and how you bake an ethos of relentless enhancement into the fabric of your data governance culture.

From Lighthouse to Continental Shelf: Adopting the Scaling Mindset

All successful Collibra implementations begin with a lighthouse project, a contained use case that delivers tangible value quickly. The energy around that use case is intense and focused, almost intimate. You know the stewards by name, you attend every stand-up, you fine-tune lineage diagrams late at night because only you understand how they will be used in tomorrow's executive demo. Scaling requires you to flip that intimacy on its head. Instead of being the lone maestro, you must now orchestrate a symphony performed by dozens of conductors across multiple departments, time zones, and cultures.

The first step is mental. You stop thinking like a project manager and start thinking like a product owner for an internal platform. That shift means every new data domain becomes another customer segment with its own needs, value propositions, and adoption curve. It means you begin to measure success not by features delivered but by cumulative, compounding outcomes: how many people are finding trusted data faster, how many manual review hours have been eliminated, how many regulatory findings were averted. And most critically, it means you accept that you are never "done." The platform, the operating model, the education program—these become living products with backlogs and roadmaps that stretch indefinitely into the future.

Re-Imagining the Meta Model for the Enterprise

Remember Chapter Three, when we sweated over which asset types to include in the core meta model? Now you need to revisit those decisions with enterprise glasses on. New data domains will appear that stretch your definitions in directions you did not anticipate. Perhaps the manufacturing division wants to catalog sensor telemetry from production lines, or the marketing group needs campaign hierarchies with seasonal attributes. If your original model was rigid, cracks will show quickly.

The trick is to treat the meta model as modular. I like to picture it as a city zoning plan. The foundational zone—business terms, systems, data sets, reports—remains constant, like the downtown grid that anchors everything. Around that, you establish expansion zones where new asset types can sprout without disrupting the core. For example, you can allow a domain-specific community to extend the "Data Set" type with attributes unique to clinical trials or IoT events while still inheriting lineage and ownership relationships from the parent class.

Crucially, any modifications must pass two litmus tests: they must be semantically sound, and they must not impede performance. As your repository grows into the millions of assets, poorly designed relationships can choke graph queries or confuse nontechnical users. Before approving a meta model change, I run a "day-in-the-life" exercise. I pick a persona—say, a risk analyst in South America—and walk through how they would search, filter, and interpret the asset once the change is live. If I have to explain the design choice in person, the model is probably too complex.

Evolving the Governance Operating Model

Scaling is as much about people as technology. The tight governance council you launched with is likely composed of visionary leaders who rallied behind the lighthouse use case. As more domains come online, that council needs to morph into a federation. What does that look like in practice? You keep a central governing body—often called the Data Governance Office—that owns policy, standards, and platform funding. Surrounding it, each major business unit forms its own stewardship group with delegated authority to approve definitions, certify data quality, and escalate issues.

I learned this lesson the hard way during a global retail engagement. For the first six months, every approval in Collibra flowed through a single queue managed by a handful of enterprise stewards. When we added the merchandising domain, requests ballooned overnight and the queue backed up for weeks. Users lost faith, and usage dipped. The fix was to empower merchandising managers to approve their own terms under a policy framework we defined centrally. Within a quarter, turnaround time dropped from three weeks to three days, and demand shot up again. The moral is simple: bottlenecks are the enemy of scale, and the best way to remove them is through delegated stewardship anchored in clear policy guardrails.

Technical Scaling: Infrastructure, Performance, and Architecture Choices

As asset volumes mount, the Collibra platform moves from a boutique application to a tier-one system that underpins critical business processes. That elevation demands equal attention to performance engineering and infrastructure resilience.

If you began on the Collibra cloud, much of the horizontal scalability is handled for you, but you still need to monitor memory utilization, query latency, and background job throughput. I recommend establishing performance thresholds and alerting mechanisms that feed directly into your DevOps or Site Reliability Engineering dashboards. That way, the team responsible for keeping SAP or Salesforce online also treats Collibra as a mission-critical asset.

For on-premise or hybrid deployments, capacity planning is non-negotiable. A common mistake is to size hardware based on initial usage rather than projected growth. I know of a telecommunications client who doubled their asset count during an acquisition yet got approval for new compute nodes only after the system became painfully slow. The reputational damage took months to repair. If you anticipate aggressive growth, secure hardware budget early, and articulate the risks of under-investment in plain business language. Executives understand downtime, lost productivity, and regulatory fines far better than they understand graph database tuning.

Integration architecture also becomes more complex at scale. A handful of stitched-together ETL jobs will not suffice when you try to synchronize metadata with dozens of upstream systems. Embrace message-oriented middleware or event streaming platforms like Kafka so Collibra can ingest changes in near real time without saturating APIs. Thoughtful decoupling isolates failure domains and prevents a hiccup in one source system from cascading into your catalog.

Broadening Horizons: Adding New Data Domains and Use Cases

When scaling, you will encounter a tension between breadth and depth. Executives may push to onboard every data domain quickly to demonstrate enterprise coverage, while stewards may argue for perfecting quality controls within a single domain before moving on.

In my experience, a pragmatic middle path works best. You expand to adjacent domains that share lineage or business processes with your pilot area because they deliver immediate cross-domain value. For instance, if customer data was your starting point, marketing and sales domains are natural next steps because they reuse many of the same reference tables and ownership structures.

The real excitement comes when you jump into orthogonal domains like Supply Chain or Human Resources. Those expansions reveal the true power of an enterprise catalog: the ability to trace a compliance metric from employee records in Workday through to a financial report filed with regulators, or to link supplier quality data stored in a third-party platform back to warranty claims driving customer support volumes.

I once worked with a pharmaceutical company that began with research data. Eighteen months later they cataloged manufacturing batch records, enabling them to cut product release time by allowing QA scientists to locate specific formulation parameters in seconds instead of hours. The bridge between research and manufacturing was not obvious on day one, but the incremental wins paved the way.

Data Quality and Stewardship at Scale

In earlier chapters we set up quality rules and stewardship workflows tailored to modest asset volumes. Scaling multiplies both the volume of data quality events and the diversity of rules required.

Manual curation becomes unsustainable quickly. The antidote is twofold: automation and risk-based prioritization.

Automation means programmatic rule creation, evaluation, and result ingestion. If you have a data quality tool that already flags anomalies, integrate its output directly into Collibra issues, linking them to the affected data sets without human intervention. Then design workflows that notify stewards only when severity crosses a threshold, freeing them from triaging every minor blip.

Risk-based prioritization relies on metadata itself. Criticality scores, sensitivity classifications, and usage metrics combine to surface quality issues that truly matter. A misspelling in an internal training spreadsheet may never bubble to the top, while a missing foreign key in a high-volume billing table triggers immediate escalation. In the long run, steward burnout is avoided, because effort aligns with business impact.

Harnessing Automation, AI, and Machine Learning

The industry buzz around active metadata and intelligent governance has substance. Modern Collibra releases support automated/assisted lineage and classification (often ML-assisted via scanners/connectors) and rich usage analytics. Where ML isn't native, partner tools can supply it. To scale efficiently, you should exploit these capabilities rather than clinging to manual curation out of habit.

Take lineage as an example. Early pilots often involve manually drawn diagrams to prove value. At scale, you lean on automated parsers that crawl SQL scripts, ETL packages, or BI tool semantic layers. The extracted lineage is not always perfect, but even a baseline generates discovery benefits for users. You can layer manual refinement on top of the machine-generated skeleton, concentrating human effort where it adds the most trust.

AI-assisted data classification is another gem. One financial services client fed Collibra's automatic classification engine thousands of sample records labeled for personally identifiable information. Within weeks, they had a high-fidelity model that could flag PII in previously undocumented tables across regions, accelerating GDPR compliance and saving millions of euros in potential fines.

These tools might feel experimental during a pilot, but at scale they become the backbone of sustainable governance. Embrace them early, iterate, and disseminate success stories to foster adoption.

Establishing a Continuous Improvement Loop

Traditional project management concludes with a closure phase. Governance, as I have stressed, does not. You need a continuous improvement loop that combines metrics, retrospectives, and roadmap planning in a cadence that matches your enterprise rhythm.

Metrics come first. In Chapter Thirteen we covered KPI

development—usage statistics, publishing velocity, data quality scores, issue resolution times. Once you have baseline values, you schedule quarterly or bi-annual health checks. During these sessions you ask a simple question: are the numbers trending toward your target outcomes? If not, what impediments exist?

Retrospectives borrow from agile software delivery. Every implementation team—central and domain-specific—meets periodically to discuss what is working, what is not, and what actions they will take to improve. The best retrospectives I have witnessed happen in person at least once a year, often tied to a Data Governance Summit or Community of Practice meeting. Stakeholders get out of their silos, share war stories, and build relationships that grease the wheels of cross-domain collaboration.

Finally, you integrate lessons learned into the roadmap. I prefer a rolling twelve-month horizon, with features, integrations, and training initiatives prioritized according to value and feasibility. The roadmap is published in Collibra itself, reinforcing transparency and inviting feedback directly from platform users.

Advanced Workflows and Federated Governance

As adoption spreads, your workflow inventory will balloon. The basic data set approval you built during sprint three might remain, but you will introduce specialized flows for exceptions like emergency data releases or regulatory attestations that bypass normal sequences under strict conditions.

Federated governance helps prevent workflow sprawl from descending into chaos. You define a catalog of standard workflow templates centrally, each tagged with usage guidelines and escalation policies. Domain teams clone these templates and tweak parameters—say, approvers or SLA durations—without altering the underlying process logic. The result is local flexibility within a global framework.

One multinational I assisted achieved remarkable efficiency by building a "workflow factory." A small automation squad inside the Data Governance Office used Collibra's BPMN engine and API connectors to roll out new workflows in days, with central template/version control and pre-prod regression tests, driven by a prioritized domain backlog. The factory approach kept development quality high, avoided duplicative effort, and provided a clear point of escalation for maintenance.

Sustaining User Adoption for the Long Haul

User adoption does not peak and plateau. It fluctuates as employees join, leave, or switch roles. New tools emerge, organizational objectives pivot, and attention spans wander. Your challenge is to weave Collibra into the daily fabric of the enterprise so thoroughly that abandoning it becomes inconceivable.

I like to think of adoption as a three-legged stool: education, engagement, and reinforcement. Education includes formal training sessions, self-paced tutorials, and contextual help embedded directly inside Collibra. Engagement comes from storytelling—broadcasting success stories through newsletters, town halls, and intranet articles that spotlight individuals who solved real problems using the catalog. Reinforcement requires policy levers; for example, mandating that all new data projects document assets in Collibra before moving to production, or integrating Collibra search into your BI portal so users discover assets organically rather than through a separate login.

An anecdote from my consulting travels underscores the importance of reinforcement. At a media company, leadership rolled out Collibra with a splashy launch but allowed new data projects to bypass documentation if timelines were tight. Predictably, teams claimed urgency on nearly every project, and adoption stagnated. Only after the CIO issued a simple directive—no production deployment without a Collibra lineage diagram—did compliance and therefore usage shoot up. The platform transitioned from optional to indispensable overnight, without heavy-handed policing.

Iterative Change Management

Scaling and continuous improvement are change management journeys, each iteration introducing new capabilities and requiring renewed buy-in. The ADKAR model—Awareness, Desire, Knowledge, Ability, Reinforcement—has served me well across multiple programs. You revisit each element whenever you roll out a sizable enhancement.

Take the introduction of automated classification. First, create Awareness via a live demo illustrating how the feature identifies sensitive data. Spark Desire by sharing metrics on manual tagging effort saved in the pilot. Provide Knowledge through step-by-step guides. Ensure Ability by offering office hours where stewards can test the model on their own datasets. Finally, drive Reinforcement by publicizing early wins and integrating classification metrics into stewardship performance reviews.

Applying such structured change management repeatedly might feel tedious, but it prevents the misalignment and resistance that often undercut scaling efforts.

Securing Funding and Executive Sponsorship

Continuous improvement costs money—licensing, infrastructure, dedicated headcount—yet governance programs often struggle to compete with high-visibility revenue projects. Your most powerful ally is quantified value. Earlier chapters taught you to track KPIs; now you convert those into monetary benefits. Faster onboarding of new data sources saves man-hours; reduced duplication of reports cuts infrastructure spend; improved compliance averts fines. Package these outcomes into concise, visually compelling storytelling for executive stakeholders.

I still remember the quarterly steering committee meeting when a Fortune 50 CFO looked at a single slide showing that Collibra-enabled lineage let auditors trace revenue calculations in minutes rather than days. He turned to his controller and said, "Make sure this team never runs out of budget." That endorsement secured funding not just for another year but for a multiyear roadmap including AI and self-service analytics integrations.

Navigating Globalization and Regulatory Complexity

Scaling across regions introduces localization, language considerations, and divergent regulatory regimes. Collibra's community and domain structure helps, but you must configure it thoughtfully. For example, a global bank might set up regional communities like EMEA, APAC, and Americas, each governed by localized data protection policies. Shared assets then sit in a global domain referenced by all regions, ensuring consistent definitions while allowing local compliance nuances.

Language can be tricky. Collibra supports UI localization and you can model multilingual terms via alternate names/synonyms. With proper synonyms/aliases, search works in either language. In Europe, I encountered a situation where French stewards refused to adopt English-only terms, while the corporate office insisted on a single language for regulatory submissions. We solved it by storing English as the primary label and French as an alternate. Search indexing allowed queries in either language, and stewards could toggle their preferred display. This compromise preserved global consistency without alienating local users.

Case Study: A Financial Giant's Journey from Twelve to Ten Thousand Users

Let me take you behind the scenes of a bank I worked with for four years. We started with a single domain—risk analytics—serving twelve risk managers. The initial goal was to standardize glossary terms for Basel regulatory reporting. Results were promising: the first audit cycle closed with zero data definition findings, a bank record.

Eighteen months later, the catalog housed 40,000 assets across Finance, Operations, and Treasury. But performance lagged, adoption plateaued, and the steering committee questioned further investment. We realized that our centralized approval workflow had become a choke point. Every new term, table, or report needed blessing from the same overworked steward group. Average approval time ballooned to thirty-seven days, infuriating users.

We pivoted. A federated model granted each division its own stewardship panel with predefined approval criteria. Central governance retained veto power for cross-division definitions but delegated everyday decisions locally. We also migrated from on-premise to Collibra cloud, boosting performance. Six months post-pivot, user base jumped to ten thousand, approval time dropped to eight days, and the catalog grew to 250,000 assets. The program now runs with a hybrid funding model: centralized budget for core platform, divisional chargebacks for specialty integrations.

Case Study: Healthcare System Spanning Clinical and Research Data

A large academic medical center approached scaling from a different angle. Their lighthouse use case cataloged clinical trial data for FDA compliance. Researchers soon wanted genomic and imaging datasets linked to trial protocols. The challenge was sensitivity and consent management. Certain genomic attributes could not be exposed to all researchers without additional patient consent.

We leveraged fine-grained permissions on assets/attribute types and lineage views. Dynamic access policies synced from the consent system-controlled metadata visibility (including lineage nodes). The platform integrated with an enterprise consent management system; updates flowed through REST APIs, revoking or granting access automatically.

To sustain continuous improvement, the center established a monthly "Data Governance Grand Rounds," mirroring the medical tradition of case presentation. Each session highlighted a governance win—like speeding up IRB approval by referencing standardized study metadata—and a governance failure—such as a lineage gap that delayed drug safety reporting. The storytelling format resonated with clinicians, and the program scaled to thousands of users, bridging clinical and research data while maintaining ironclad privacy controls.

Avoiding Scaling Anti-Patterns

No scaling chapter is complete without confession. I have fallen into traps, and you might too. One anti-pattern is the "Big Bang Domain Launch," where enthusiastic executives demand simultaneous onboarding of every data source. Integration teams drown, lineage diagrams become incomprehensible, and user trust erodes. Successful programs instead use rolling waves, stabilizing one domain before absorbing the next.

Another pitfall is the "Governance Priesthood," a small elite group who guard the platform zealously, rejecting any suggestion they did not author. This behavior alienates potential contributors and suffocates innovation. Counteract it by celebrating external contributions, publishing open guidelines, and rotating stewardship duties to avoid empire-building.

Finally, beware "Tool Worship." Collibra is powerful, but it cannot fix broken processes or dysfunctional cultures on its own. I once consulted for an organization that spent seven figures on licensing and integration yet refused to assign data owners because "everyone is responsible." The catalog filled with unowned, outdated assets, and users abandoned it. We fixed the problem only after redefining accountability matrices and linking data ownership to performance metrics.

The Continuous Improvement Mindset: Culture Eats Roadmaps for Breakfast

Peter Drucker's adage that culture eats strategy for breakfast applies doubly to data governance. You can craft the most elegant scaling roadmap, deploy AI classifiers, and design dashboards that sparkle like Vegas billboards, but unless the organization internalizes the belief that data governance is essential to its mission, improvements will stall.

Culture change manifests in small rituals: a product manager pastes a Collibra asset link into a Slack thread without prompting; an analyst starts her presentation by citing the certified metrics she pulled from the catalog; a new hire receives Collibra training during orientation next to cybersecurity briefings. These micro-moments signal to everyone that governed data is the default, not the exception.

To cultivate that culture, keep telling stories, keep rewarding collaboration, and keep showing tangible outcomes. Celebrate the first time a legal dispute is resolved because lineage proved data authenticity. Highlight when machine-learning model turnaround time shrinks thanks to self-service discovery. Over time, sustained cheerleading evolves into embedded values, and continuous improvement becomes second nature.

Conclusion: Your Role in the Governance Journey

As we close this chapter—and this book—let me leave you with a personal reflection. I have led or advised more than forty Collibra programs across continents and industries, yet every one teaches me something new, because scaling and continuous improvement are never complete. The moment you solve one problem, another emerges. That is not a sign of failure; it is evidence of growth. Each new challenge means your organization has reached a level of maturity where finer grained issues are now visible and worthy of attention.

Your job, then, is not to chase a mythical finish line. Your job is to foster a living ecosystem where governance evolves in harmony with the business, where new ideas can be tested quickly, and where success is measured not just by dashboards but by the confidence with which people make data-driven decisions every day. If you can accomplish that—if you can make Collibra the indispensable compass that guides your organization through the fog of data complexity—then you will have built a governance program that not only scales but thrives, continuously improving as far into the future as you care to imagine. And on that morning when you open your laptop and the platform is humming, you will smile, not because the work is done, but because you know exactly how to keep making it better.

You've just walked through the same path I took on my first large-scale Collibra rollout—crash-course fundamentals, careful planning, then the steady drumbeat of agile sprints that turned blank screens into a living, breathing data governance hub. Together we looked at how a solid meta model anchors everything and how a clear operating model keeps accountability from slipping through the cracks. Every checklist and canvas in those early chapters was designed to save you from the sleepless nights I spent wondering whether I'd missed a critical dependency.

Next, we zoomed into the human side: writing user stories that actually sound like humans, lining up the right people at the right moments, and managing the emotional roller coaster that always comes with change. I've seen brilliant configurations stall because a single data steward felt left out; now you know how to avoid that. When you communicate purpose, show quick wins, and invite feedback early, momentum becomes self-propelling.

Then came the nuts and bolts—installation, integrations, workflows, automation, and all the little toggles that separate a demo environment from a production workhorse. You practiced onboarding assets at scale, wiring Collibra into your wider data ecosystem, and tracking the metrics that prove to skeptics this isn't just another shiny tool. If you take only one lesson from those chapters, let it be this: governance is a living service, and dashboards are its heartbeat.

I can still picture the day a VP stopped me in the hallway, phone in hand, showing off the lineage diagram we'd launched the week before. "I finally see where my numbers come from," she said, half amazed and half relieved. Moments like that make the late-night troubleshooting sessions worth it, and they'll happen for you, too, if you keep listening, iterating, and celebrating every insight gained. So here we are at the edge of the blank page that belongs to you alone. You have the frameworks, the stories, and the cautions; now it's your turn to turn governance from an abstract ideal into daily, visible value. Keep your meta model honest, your sprints short, and your conversations candid. If you do, Collibra won't just manage metadata—it will amplify trust in the data and in the teams who govern it.

Chapter 15 Key Terms

Continuous Improvement: An iterative approach to refining processes and outcomes over time.

Maturity Evolution: Progression through stages of governance capability and adoption.

Decentralization: Distributing governance responsibilities to domain teams rather than central control.

Retrospective Loop: Regular reflection sessions to evaluate progress and adjust direction.

Versioned Operating Model: A living governance framework that evolves through controlled updates.

Scalability: The capability of a governance program to handle growing volume and complexity.

Governance Roadmap: A strategic plan outlining the long-term development of governance capabilities.

Celebration Culture: Intentional recognition of achievements to maintain momentum and morale.

Feedback-Driven Iteration: Adjusting strategy and tooling based on stakeholder input and performance data.

Comprehensive Glossary by Discipline

Data Governance & Management

Data Governance: A framework of roles, processes, and policies ensuring that enterprise data is accurate, secure, and used responsibly.

Data Steward: The individual responsible for maintaining data quality, accuracy, and business relevance.

Data Owner: The executive accountable for a dataset's correctness, usage, and compliance.

Custodian: The technical administrator ensuring secure data storage and delivery.

Metadata: Descriptive information that explains a data element's structure, source, and purpose.

Data Lineage: A documented flow showing how data moves and transforms across systems.

Data Quality: The measure of how complete, accurate, timely, and consistent data is.

Golden Source: The authoritative version of a dataset recognized as the single source of truth.

Business Glossary: A repository of standardized business terms and definitions.

Data Asset: Any data entity with business value that requires tracking and stewardship.

Domain: A logical grouping of related data assets, usually aligned to a department or function.

Community: A high-level grouping of domains, representing broad organizational areas.

Policy: A formal rule governing how data must be managed or used.

Operating Model: The structure that defines how governance roles, responsibilities, and workflows operate.

Stewardship Council: A cross-functional group coordinating governance activities and decision-making.

Governance Charter: A document outlining purpose, scope, principles, and authority for governance.

Maturity Model: A staged framework used to evaluate an organization's governance capability.

Readiness Assessment: Evaluation of an organization's people, process, and technology before implementation.

Collibra Platform Concepts

Collibra: A data intelligence platform that enables organizations to catalog, govern, and collaborate on data.

Asset: A core Collibra object, representing any entity such as a data table, report, glossary term, or policy.

Asset Type: The category defining what kind of entity an asset is and what attributes it holds.

Attribute: A property of an asset, describing details such as owner, description, or format.

Relation: A connection between assets that defines their interdependency or lineage.

Meta Model: The blueprint that defines asset types, attributes, and relationships within Collibra.

Domain (Collibra): A container for grouping related assets within a community.

Community (Collibra): The highest organizational grouping in Collibra, representing a business area.

Workflow: An automated sequence of governance actions – such as approval, certification, or review.

Certification Workflow: A validation process that confirms a dataset meets governance requirements.

Data Catalog: Collibra's searchable inventory of data assets, enriched with metadata.

Data Lineage Harvester: A Collibra component that imports lineage metadata from external systems.

API Connector: A prebuilt integration interface that exchanges metadata between Collibra and other tools.

Operating Model (Collibra): The system of assigned roles, workflows, and accountability defined inside the platform.

Diagram View: A Collibra visualization that displays assets and their relationships as a network graph.

Governance Dashboard: A visual summary in Collibra showing data quality, stewardship activity, and KPIs.

Role-Based Access Control (RBAC): Permission system in Collibra controlling who can view or modify assets.

Agile Delivery & Project Management

Agile: An iterative project management approach emphasizing flexibility, collaboration, and continuous improvement.

Scrum: A structured agile framework built around roles, ceremonies, and sprints.

Sprint: A fixed, time-boxed period (typically 2–3 weeks) in which a defined set of tasks is completed.

Product Owner: The role responsible for maximizing product value by prioritizing the backlog.

Scrum Master: The facilitator who ensures the agile process runs smoothly and removes impediments.

Backlog: A prioritized list of work items awaiting completion.

User Story: A concise description of a feature from an end user's perspective.

Acceptance Criteria: Conditions that define when a user story is complete and acceptable.

Retrospective: A reflection session held at the end of a sprint to identify improvements.

Sprint Review: A demonstration of completed work to stakeholders at the end of a sprint.

Velocity: The amount of work completed by a team per sprint.

Definition of Done: Agreed standards that indicate when a task or deliverable is finished.

Kanban: A visual workflow management system used to improve efficiency and flow.

Regulatory & Compliance (Financial, Healthcare, Legal)

GDPR (General Data Protection Regulation): European Union law governing personal data privacy and protection.

HIPAA (Health Insurance Portability and Accountability Act): U.S. regulation ensuring privacy and security of healthcare information.

SOX (Sarbanes-Oxley Act): U.S. law enforcing accuracy and transparency in financial reporting.

Basel / BCBS 239: International banking standards requiring consistent, high-quality risk data and reporting.

KYC (Know Your Customer): Regulatory requirement for verifying customer identity in financial institutions.

AML (Anti-Money Laundering): Framework for detecting and preventing illegal financial activities.

PCI-DSS: Standard for safeguarding credit card information during processing and storage.

CCPA (California Consumer Privacy Act): U.S. law granting consumers control over personal data collected by companies.

Audit Trail: A traceable record of all governance or data actions for compliance purposes.

Regulatory Reporting: The process of producing official data reports for external regulators or authorities.

Technical & Integration Concepts

API (Application Programming Interface): A set of protocols enabling software systems to communicate and exchange data.

ETL (Extract, Transform, Load): The process of moving and transforming data between systems.

Data Warehouse: A centralized repository for structured analytical data.

Snowflake: A cloud-native data warehouse often integrated with Collibra for cataloging.

Microservices Architecture: A system design where independent services perform specific tasks and communicate via APIs.

Authentication: Verification of a user's identity before granting access.

Authorization: Determining what authenticated users are permitted to access or modify.

SaaS (Software as a Service): A software delivery model where applications are hosted and managed by a provider.

Version Control: A mechanism for tracking configuration or code changes (e.g., Git).

Automation: Use of technology to execute repetitive tasks without manual intervention.

Performance Tuning: Optimization of configurations and code for speed and efficiency.

Monitoring: Continuous tracking of system performance and health metrics.

Error Handling: Procedures to detect and manage system or integration failures.

Resilience: The ability of systems to recover quickly from disruptions.

Scalability: The capacity of systems or governance models to handle increased load or complexity.

Business Intelligence & Analytics

Business Intelligence (BI): Tools and practices for analyzing data to support decision-making.

Dashboard: A visual interface summarizing key data metrics and

KPIs.

Metric: A quantitative measure used to evaluate performance or compliance.

KPI (Key Performance Indicator): A critical metric reflecting progress toward business objectives.

Data Usage Analytics: Insights derived from how users access and apply governed data.

Cycle Time: The duration from initiation to completion of a governance or data request.

Benchmarking: Comparing performance against peers or best practices.

ROI (Return on Investment): The measurable benefit derived from a financial or strategic investment.

Change Management & Adoption

Change Management: The discipline of preparing, supporting, and helping individuals adopt change.

User Adoption: The degree to which users embrace new tools or processes.

Change Resistance: Behavioral reluctance to adapt to new systems or governance frameworks.

Executive Sponsorship: Senior leadership support that legitimizes and funds governance initiatives.

Communication Plan: A structured approach to informing and engaging stakeholders.

Training Plan: A roadmap for educating users on new systems or processes.

Awareness Campaign: Initiatives to promote visibility and excitement around governance programs.

Recognition Program: A formal system for rewarding active contributors and stewards.

Cultural Inertia: Organizational tendency to revert to legacy behaviors and systems.

Feedback Loop: Continuous input and improvement mechanism based on user experience.

Continuous Improvement: Ongoing refinement of processes and culture based on lessons learned.

Celebration Culture: The intentional recognition of progress to sustain motivation and engagement.

Data Ethics & Risk Management

Data Ethics: The practice of ensuring data is collected, managed, and used in ways that align with moral principles such as fairness, transparency, and respect for individual rights.

Responsible AI: The application of artificial intelligence systems that adhere to ethical standards, ensuring fairness, explainability, and the avoidance of unintended harm.

Data Privacy: The right of individuals and organizations to control how personal or sensitive information is collected, shared, and used.

Bias Mitigation: The process of identifying and correcting unfair or unbalanced outcomes in data collection, modeling, or interpretation.

Data Protection: Policies and technical controls designed to safeguard personal and sensitive data from unauthorized access or misuse.

Risk Assessment: A systematic evaluation of potential threats to data security, privacy, or governance objectives.

Data Classification: The process of labeling data according to its sensitivity or business criticality to determine access and handling requirements.

Access Control: Mechanisms that regulate who can view, modify, or delete data assets based on defined roles or permissions.

Consent Management: The documentation and enforcement of users' permissions for how their personal data may be collected and used.

Audit Trail: A chronological record of system activities, allowing verification of who accessed or modified data.

Incident Response: A structured process for detecting, managing, and recovering from security or data integrity breaches.

Data Retention Policy: Guidelines defining how long data should be stored, archived, or deleted to meet legal and business requirements.

Governance Risk and Compliance (GRC): An integrated approach aligning governance policies, risk management, and regulatory compliance into a cohesive framework.

Ethical Stewardship: The responsibility of data professionals to act with integrity, balancing business benefit with societal impact.

Transparency: The commitment to openly documenting how data is sourced, processed, and used so stakeholders can evaluate its trustworthiness.

Anonymization: The transformation of data to prevent identification of individuals while preserving analytical value.

Data Sovereignty: The principle that data is subject to the laws and governance structures of the country where it is collected or stored.

Security Governance: The coordination of policies and roles that ensure data assets are protected and used responsibly throughout their lifecycle.

Privacy Impact Assessment (PIA): An analysis conducted before deploying new data processes or systems to understand their privacy implications and mitigate risks.

Alphabetical Index of Key Terms

Use this index to quickly locate which glossary section contains the definition for each term. Terms are grouped by discipline such as Data Governance & Management, Collibra Platform Concepts, Agile Delivery & Project Management, Regulatory & Compliance, Technical & Integration, Business Intelligence & Analytics, Change Management & Adoption, or Data Ethics & Risk Management.

A

D

F

H

I

K

L

M

O

P

Q

R

S

T

U

V

W

www.ingramcontent.com/pod-product-compliance
Lightning Source LLC
LaVergne TN
LVHW080026210926
848481LV00011B/3114